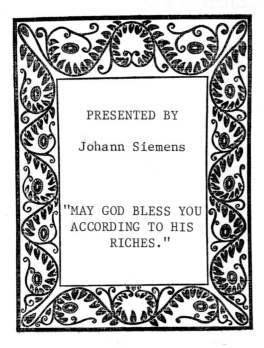

The Wheel and the Cross

The Wheel
and the
Cross

A Christian Response to
the Technological Revolution

by

WALDO BEACH

John Knox Press
ATLANTA

Library of Congress Cataloging in Publication Data

Beach, Waldo.
     The wheel and the cross.

     Includes bibliographical references and index.
     1. Christian ethics.   2. Church and the world.
I.   Title.
BJ1251.B37   241   79-87738
ISBN 0-8042-0866-2

Contents

Introduction

This is a book about Christian ethics, which, defined in simplest terms, means the moral norms of Christian living as found in Scripture and tradition. It is addresssd to those who search for Christian solutions to the ethical problems that arise in today's technological society. It invites you to explore with me in some systematic way—perhaps in an adult church school class, perhaps in an introductory undergraduate course in Christian social ethics—the many conflicts that appear when the moral demands of the cross of Christ go counter to the requirements of life run by the wheel, the symbol of technology. It also invites you to consider and compare traditional and contemporary secular moralities and to think carefully about those ways faithful to the cross that can be lived out in a world radically and permanently altered by human inventions and machineries. Certain truths must stand strong and steady against change, but others must bend to fit the needs of the times. Who is to decide which are permanent and which flexible?

What resources I may bring as guide in this search derive from many years of teaching Christian ethics in a university seminary, where men and women are equipped for various forms of ministry, some within church pastorates as conventionally defined, some outside. But these are more than formal academic exercises tainted with the musty odor of the classroom. They also express reflections upon personal experiences as a husband and father, as a producer and consumer, as a citizen and voter, where one is forced to wrestle daily against "the principalities and powers" with at least a measure of faithful integrity.

The book is therefore neither a detailed textbook, heavy-laden with scholarly apparatus, nor a scholarly treatise for scholars. It is beamed toward the Christian lay person who may have no formal theological education. On the other hand, it is not intended as an evangelical tract, certainly not one offering instant salvation in ten easy steps. You will find in its pages often more grope than grasp. But it is offered as an invitation to study and discuss the formidable challenge which technology poses for one of Christian conscience. It is offered also in the confidence that, even as the wheels spin faster and faster, it is possible to live within their whir obedient to what the cross signifies.

I would like to express indebtedness to the faculty of Fuller Theological Seminary, Pasadena, California for the privilege of giving the Jaymes P. Morgan Lectures, wherein some of the seminal ideas of this book were proposed. A word of thanks is also due to various graduate students and faculty colleagues at Duke University, especially in the sciences, who gently set me straight on technical facts where I went astray in the pathless jungle of information: in particular, Janet McDowell, Henry Fairbank, Roger Anderson, John Westerhoff, and Nancy Fulcher.

1

The Worship
of the Wheel

This is the greatest week in the history of the world since
the creation.
            Richard M. Nixon, commenting on the successful
                        mission of Apollo 11, July 1969

"Let us stand and sing Hymn #348, 'Faith of our Fathers! Living Still,' though we all know it's really almost dead." If the pastor
should announce the hymn this way during the worship service, it
would send more than a mild tremor through the congregation. But
would it not be correct?

American culture is increasingly secular. There are many clear
signals of a process of secularization: the decrease in church attendance and support, at least in the mainline churches, Protestant and
Catholic; the growing religious illiteracy among the products of
public education, where separation of church and state precludes religious instruction; and the shift from a substantive to a merely cere-
monial and perfunctory meaning attached to Christian symbols in
public exercises, where the solemn words of the invocation opening a
session of congress are quite forgotten when the real substance of the
secular agenda is addressed. Policy is rarely framed out of prayer. All
point with alarm to the sharp rise in the crime rate in America. Rape,
murder, arson, burglary, the breakdown of law and order are ex-
plained as the direct and dark result of a decline of religious faith. And not only "raw" street crime, but even more seriously
the polite white-collar crimes in the business and political communi-
ties up to the very top, where power and expediency rather than
integrity become the rules of action, are credited to a loss of our
inner sense of accountability and conscience rooted in religious faith.

The traditional bulwarks are crumbling. America is becoming a secular, faithless culture.

We must set aside here consideration of the intriguing question as to whether "our fathers" were indeed as faithful as we depict them in our rural nostalgia for the "good old days," or whether political or business scandals, in high places and low, were as prevalent then as they are now. An unsentimental rereading of our history might correct our "Currier and Ives" illusion and remind us that history is always a morally ambiguous mixture of good and evil. But although human practices are forever a faulty expression of ideals, the generalization does seem to stand that the traditional religious ideals which nurtured the American experiment no longer have the authority and aura of sanctity that once they held. In that sense, we do live in a "secular" America or what is called a "post-Christian" era.

But this common reading of the process of "secularization" is quite too simple and facile. Indeed, it would distort the story of religion in America to tell it as a decline and fall of faith, the erosion of religion, the slide from faithfulness to faithlessness. The process of secularization is much more involved than that. Essentially, it is not the disappearance of faith, but a transfer of loyalty and trust from the traditional objects of faith, in this case the transcendent God of the Hebrew-Christian religion, to *new* objects of ultimate loyalty and trust. People are no more or less "religious" than they ever were; the shift is in the gods whom they worship and obey and count on to give meaning and direction to their lives. While the "official" or "church" religions of America remain Judaism or one or another of the various versions of Christianity, the "real" religion, or the "invisible" religion, that commands the loyalty and devotion of the heart may be one of a number of secular faiths.

Working with this more subtle meaning of the process of secularization, we can more readily see that in large measure Americans are practicing polytheists, with a whole pantheon of gods. These deities may not appear as the official gods. They may be quite everyday and mundane, as near as the microwave oven or as far as the astronaut's TV camera on the moon. But they become sacralized and take on an aura of sanctity, like the soft radiant light around the head of the beautiful young wife advertising Geritol, a halo every bit as numinous as that over a Francesca madonna.

In the Western world there are several secular religions which might be examined, were there time, each one with its own theology and ethics, its cultic rites, its priests and prophets, its saints and seers, and many devout worshipers. Free-enterprise capitalism is one such secular faith. Communism is another, though for the American not the live option it is for a citizen of Italy or France. Or "civil religion" which in its American form is the celebration of the American way of life as supreme, the only sure path to salvation, not only for Americans, but for the world. Americans are God's chosen people.

The Religion of Scientism

For the purposes of this study, however, the focus is on the religion of scientism, certainly one of the most powerful gods in the secular pantheon. How it came to its throne, through the long history of the rise of science in Western Europe with its tangled roots that reach back into the Biblical world view and into the Renaissance, how it developed with the various breakthroughs starting in the seventeenth century linked with such names as Galileo, Newton, Bacon, Descartes, Darwin, and Einstein, how it gradually became the established church in common culture, how scientific theory was put to practical uses in technology (which simply defined means "applied science")—all these are not my concern here. Suffice it to say that Western civilization has journeyed over a great Continental Divide of thought. The scientific revolution has moved us today into a radically different frame of mind from that of Biblical times.

Technology has not only changed the face of the earth; it has changed the human heart. In Biblical culture, the fundamental stance of a person, normatively, the relation felt to his or her universe, was that of reverence, the fear of the Lord. All human responses to the world of nature were surrounded and obliged by that sense of reverence for the One who created heaven and earth "and the fulness thereof."

Over twenty centuries, by slow degrees, this attitude of wonder and awe has gradually shifted to that of curiosity, where the self rises from prayer, begins to probe into the mysteries, to ask "how" do things happen, what are the immanent laws that account for the regularities of natural happenings, whether they be the wheeling of the stars or the growth of snails. Explanation dispels the *mysterium tremendum*. Nature is "desacralized." Once the "how" of things is understood, in cause-effect sequence, it is not then far to human intervention in the manipulation of nature to serve whatever needs are taken as desirable. At the beginning of this saga, people in prayer, in the fear of the Lord, covenanted "to till . . . and to keep" the garden of nature. At the end: *homo faber*, man as technician, uses nature as he wills.

Every serious religion has a certain syndrome of beliefs, those value-systems and the faith-premises that underlie them which constitute its "systematic theology." Even though for scientism there has been no major theologian to write out a three-volume system, and though all of the following articles of faith are sharply disputed among scientists, one can sketch (using Christian categories) the systematic faith of the religion of scientism in its popular forms as follows:

a. The Theory of Knowledge (or Epistemology)

For scientism, the way to the truth is by inductive reasoning upon hard empirical data, leading to hypotheses which then are further tested in research, so that tentative generalized conclusions may be drawn about what factors can be counted on to cause certain effects. The final truth is never in, to be sure, for new findings may upset old theories, but one thing is sure: this is the *only* way to whatever certainties we have, whether they be about the movement of the tides or the moods of the soul.

b. The Nature of Ultimate Reality (Metaphysics or Ontology)

Should you ask a white-coated scientist: "What is the ultimate stuff from whence all the phenomena of nature are made?" you are likely to get in reply a polite excuse from an answer; for the scientist's tunnel-vision preoccupation with cells, steam pressure, neurons, or neuroses is likely to prevent any vision of the whole. The scientist will simply say, with a shrug, "Who knows?" But if pressed, the likely scientific surmise would be that ultimate reality is matter in motion, a "blind fortuitous concourse of atoms." Whether that be energy in the cloak of matter or matter infused with energy, in either case the universe is not the awesome handiwork of a creator God, whose beneficent will gives it design, symmetry, beauty, goodness. It is morally neutral.

c. The View of Human Nature (Anthropology)

What is it that distinguishes human beings from animals? A glance at one's fingernails and toenails, plus a quick visit to the zoo, gives sufficient evidence of our simian ancestry. Though there are clear affinities between animal and human behavior, there is a qualitative gap between even the highest form of animal life and human life. Though it may seem presumptuous to say so, only human beings are self-conscious, gifted with memory and foresight, and capable of intelligence. *Homo sapiens:* the human creature capable of thought. One of the chief articles of faith in the creed of scientism is that we are *homo faber,* a race of tool-users. In scientism, *sapiens*—wisdom— does not connote the contemplation of Pure Ideas, as for Plato, nor reverence of the Lord, which for the psalmist was the beginning of wisdom. Rather, human intelligence means ingenuity in devising and using tools to cope with the natural environment.

d. Salvation (or Soteriology)

The classic Christian scenario pictures the human condition as being far east of Eden, where, since the "fall," the human predicament of sin, as "pride" *(hubris),* alienating us from both God and neighbor, is one from which we may be saved only by the grace of God, present crucially in the figure of Jesus Christ. Scientism replaces this sin-salvation scenario with another: problem-solution. The human predicament is that of some provisional maladjustment or human dysfunctioning in relation to nature, or in society, or within ourselves. "Salvation" lies by way of the discovery and use of some technique that can restore right functioning. For there is no problem incapable of solution by human cleverness—technique becomes then "the means of grace and the hope of glory."

e. The Pattern of History and Its Goal (Eschatology)

In scientism the whole human story is not one of random chaos, or of endless, weary, cyclical repetition, but of progress from the prescientific past of primitive history through the discovery and employment of scientific means moving ever upward toward a utopia of perfect attunement of ourselves with nature and with neighbor. Since the growth of scientific research and know-how is cumulative, we live in the confidence that history is progressive. Yes, there are setbacks, but taken in the long overview, the human story is one of the gradual triumph of human intelligence and technique over every problem on earth. (And in this space age, even the sky is no limit to scientific reach.)

The "center" of history, as the symbolic point where the clue as to its meaning is revealed, can therefore be said to be "the wheel," symbolizing that crucial device whereby people were liberated from prescientific existence and by technique empowered to the realization of their true destiny.

It should be noted in passing, that this optimistic doctrine of progress, almost taken for granted through the last part of the nineteenth century up until World War I, is no longer a confident article of faith among philosophers of science at the present time. In fact, it is from the scientists themselves, physicists and biochemists, that we hear prophecies of doom, foretelling catastrophe ahead if we continue to perfect weapons of mass destruction and ecological plunder. The moral ambiguities of scientific successes come to light, for as often as not a "solution" may bring in its wake side effects that pose new perils and problems, as in some "cures" of medical science. But popular science continues to hold fast its faith that technical skill can and will solve every human problem and improve the quality and quantity of life for all. In the wheel we trust. It will empower us to prevail.

f. Ethics

From these faith-premises about the nature of ultimate reality, of humanity, and of history, the ethics of scientism follows directly. The measure of moral worth is efficiency. The Great Commandment, the first law of all, is no longer the love of God and neighbor. Rather it reads: Be Efficient. For the pragmatic perfection of technique in maximizing human speed, power, convenience, comfort—that is the moral purpose of existence. At the Last Judgment (or in the scientist's translation: in the Final Analysis) the crucial question put to you will not be: were you faithful, or did you love your neighbor as Christ loved you, but: were you efficient in your life-style?

As I have said, no *Summa Theologica* has yet spelled out this system of faith, and all of these doctrines are sharply disputed, both from within and outside of the scientific community. Yet in our Western consciousness these constitute a syndrome of faith-premises that permeate and give warrant to most of our activity.

Its doxology might be sung: "Glory be to the Father, Science, and to the Son, Technology, and to the Holy Spirit of Efficiency, which, although it was not in the beginning, surely is now, and ever shall be, world without end. Amen."

A creedal form of this faith might read:

> I believe in humanity almighty, remaker of earth and explorer of heaven, who through the discovery and use of the wheel has set itself on the road toward perfect adjustment. I believe there are no limits to growth, no problems insoluble by human ingenuity, and I look in hope toward that perfection of human happiness on earth which is life everlasting.

Would it be fair to say that this creed would make more sense to some of the Middle Americans than the Apostles' Creed which they perfunctorily mumble in church on Sunday?

All religions, of course, become institutionalized, with their churches, priests and pastors, cultic rites and traditions, ceremonies and sacraments. No less is this true for the religion of scientism. True, there are other secular deities celebrated and adored in American culture, like capitalism, or "Americanity." In the daily devotional exercises of the American, scientism, capitalism, and Americanity are often mixed together. Through the mass media, especially TV, the high priests of scientism and capitalism offer in matins and evensongs the sacraments of grace to the devout. What Xerox can perform is pronounced "a miracle" (even by a Catholic monk). Salvation from acid indigestion or "slight irregularity" is realized by Di-Gel or M-O laxative; the drama of alienation and reconciliation is enacted in ten seconds. Aspirin is "recommended by leading doctors, 3 to 1." (Who decides that they are "leading" doctors?) "Union Carbide. Today something we do will touch your life." We are almost prompted to kneel in reverence and say, *"Kyrie eleison,* Union Carbide. *Adoramus Te."* The point to note in all this solemn hocus-pocus is that these rituals insinuate constantly into our souls the belief that technology is the savior for all human problems, that human happiness is accessible just by employing this handy device, available at your local drugstore.

I have claimed that whereas the "official" or nominal religion of America is Judaism or Christianity, the real religion is scientism. But I cannot leave the matter at that. There is trouble in the soul of the American, of which he or she may be hardly conscious, that arises from the tension and contradictions between these two faith-systems. By the very monopolistic nature of these opposed faiths, it is impossible to hold them together at once. They jostle one another for sovereignty. How to reconcile one with the other? There are several attractive ways.

One is to convert Christianity to scientism, i. e., to call all Christian doctrines and practices however old and venerable before the bar of scientific truth. In that Supreme Court, if they can be demonstrated as useful or "relevant" in aiding efficient living, they are valid. Thus, prayer is treated as a useful therapy in gaining peace of mind (so: "Dial-a-Prayer"). TM offers its salvific fixes. Christian love is an effective device for converting enemies to friendliness. Faith even in such a "myth" as Providence may be a useful therapy to depression. The test of truth here is a pragmatic one: does it work in achieving optimum adjustment?

Another enticing way to resolve the tension between the Hebrew-Christian faith and scientism is to escape the technocratic society and all its values and retreat into the safe confines of a simple Biblical faith. This way not only protests the idolatry of scientism in the name of the God of the Christian faith, but rejects technology and all its fruits as works of the Devil. Let us go pretechnological. Back to the Bible. The resurgence of fundamentalism and neo-evangelical churches in the latter part of the twentieth century, among the young and old, is a sign of the popularity of this way of coping with the tension. But to try to go pretechnological is romantic and impossible. To turn one's mind against all that scientific discovery has provided in a revision of our world view is foolish indeed. It would be like reverting to a Biblical cosmology of a three-storied universe: earth as a narrow flat plane, with heaven above and hell below, as the frame in which to set the human enterprise.

Perhaps the most convenient way to cope with the tension between scientism and Christianity is to try to escape it by dividing existence into the Sunday compartment, where we subscribe with more or less ardor to the articles of the Christian faith, under the sign of the cross, and the weekday compartment, where we live by the articles of the scientistic faith, under the sign of the wheel. And just don't worry if these faith-systems and life-styles are not consonant.

The Integrity of Faith

But for the long pull, none of these "resolutions" of the tension will do. Something in us demands an integrity of mind and heart, that we try to "get it all together" in a coherent way. Neither a conversion of Christianity into scientism, nor the rejection of science and technology, nor a split-level house of faith, with Christianity on one level, scientism on another, serves to provide human life with an integral frame of reference needful for Christian living in a technocratic age.

Preferably, the point of view proposed, and spelled out in the following chapters, is that of "radical monotheism," the primal faith in a transcendent, benevolent, governing will, the One behind all the many, who creates and sustains, who judges and redeems, the nature of whose gracious will is crucially known in the event of Jesus Christ. The primal affirmation of radical monotheism is this: " 'Hear, O Israel': The LORD our God is one,' " and, as Jesus repeats it in the Great Commandment, " 'You shall love the Lord your God with all your heart, and with all your soul, and with all your mind. . . . And . . . You shall love your neighbor as yourself.' "

God is a jealous God. "Him only shalt thou serve." (KJV) The worship of science is then a form of idolatry, which means, as St. Augustine put it, to place infinite trust in something finite, or to treat as God some limited part of the order of creation.

The stance of the Christian toward science and technology, therefore, is neither dread nor worship of technology, neither technophobia nor technolatry. Rather, it is to see all that science and technology have provided as potential means for good *or* evil ends. But technicians alone are not in a position to decide about the quality of the ends; that is a moral choice. The Christian criterion brought to every technological decision is this: will the use of this machinery or technique serve more to brutalize or to humanize existence? And the criterion for *that* the Christian would derive from the mind of Christ. The right relation of science and Christianity, then, is to be defined not as redemption *from* technology but as the redemption *of* technology, by recovering the right relation of means and ends, by using the wheel to serve the ethical ends of the cross, in short, to love God and neighbor efficiently. These matters point us toward a normative statement of Christian ethical theory to be spelled out in the next chapter.

2

From Christian Love
to Social Policy

> Justice degenerates into mere order without justice if the
> pull of love is not upon it.
>
> *Reinhold Niebuhr*

From the description of the technological society in chapter 1 and of the hidden secular religion that empowers its machinery, we turn to consider the Christian ethical norms relevant to choices and decisions to be made in a technological age. For many, it would appear that we move from complex problems to simple answers. The Christian life means being kind and nice. It means loving God and neighbor. It means giving your heart to the Lord Jesus. It means doing what Christ would do. So the preacher prescribes, and so we pray that "thy will be done on earth, as it is in heaven."

But it does not take much thought to realize how far it is from heaven to earth and how remote from the tangle of decisions in life these simple norms are. The counsels and commands from the pulpit to live and act in a Christ-like way, however earnest, sail gently right over the problems and dilemmas in the hearts and minds of those who sit in the pews. What is the *content* of God's will? "Love thy neighbor as thyself." (KJV) Fine. But *which* neighbor is to be served, among the competing neighbor claims and needs that batter my conscience, where it is impossible to serve them all? Just around the house, the problems of ethical choice are rarely simple. But this ambiguity of circumstance is especially evident in decisions of public policy, in economics and politics, domestic and international, where a welter of competing needs and wants, licit and illicit, converge at the vortex of my choices as citizen, or as producer and consumer. To

be suitable to such dilemmas of choice, a more careful explication of
Christian ethical norms is needed.

Beyond Legalism and Lawlessness

One venerable tradition in the long history of Christian ethics
addressed to this problem is that of *legalism*. For those who live by
this tradition, the will of God is spelled out in particulars. This may
be in terms of prohibitions, such as in the Decalogue, or of specified
virtues: love, truthfulness, patience, trust, etc. In Catholic moral theory, as it comes to flower in medieval thought, the principles of "natural law" became the basis of quite detailed guidance for the
Christian. "Natural law" means the enactment of God's eternal laws
in the created world and there discernible by human reason, even
apart from revelation. Such principles as "private property for common use," or the obligation and rights of persons in a monogamous
relationship to have children and raise them in the true faith, are still
the ethical basis of current Catholic policy. In the Protestant tradition, the Bible is taken as the lawbook where the specific contents of
the will of God are both "shown and commanded." And in Protestant ethical history, there have been many guides to the Christian
conscience, books of casuistry on how to choose in this or that situation.

But there are difficulties with legalism of any sort. When the good
life is defined as a laundry list of dos and don'ts, persons may come to
obey the letter of the law, but neglect—even violate—the spirit of the
law, as Jesus himself pointed up in his running debate with the Pharisees, the legalists of his day. Moreover, particular laws framed for
one age may no longer be applicable to a later culture radically
changed. For example, the Roman Catholic theory of the "just" war,
framed by Augustine and Thomas Aquinas in the days of swords and
shields, is now rendered obsolete by technology and weapons of mass
destruction they could not even imagine. With modern weaponry it
is impossible to wage war "in a just manner." Many other features of
natural-law ethics, and of Biblical moral mandates, seem decrepit
anachronisms in a technocratic age. What Biblical verse could provide guidance directly for decisions to be made at MIT about DNA

research, or that a president—even a devout Baptist who reads his Bible regularly—must make about nuclear proliferation or the neutron bomb?

Partly in protest against the obsolescence and confinement of legalism, there has arisen recently a completely opposite popular style of "doing" ethics, called "situation ethics." In light of the unprecedented character of contemporary moral problems, since "New occasions teach new duties; Time makes ancient good uncouth," the advocates of situation ethics ask that the Christian address these novel problems armed only with a single, simple intent: to love. Let love improvise on the spot, turning love this way or that as the situation requires, setting aside "principles" if need be, that persons may be served. As spelled out by its leading proponent, Joseph Fletcher, the single Christian virtue of love *(agape)* is as relevant to policy formation, where the good for groups or classes of neighbors is at stake, as it is for single one-to-one neighbor relations, "for justice is love distributed, nothing else."[1]

Although situation ethics seems at first contact to be a welcome brisk wind, blowing away all the restrictions of decrepit laws, yet on close examination it proves as vulnerable in its way as the legalism it would displace. To trust love alone to improvise policies, on the spot, that can serve the common good is much too naive. Christian justice is more than just the multiplication of love from one-on-one to many-on-many neighbor relations. In short, more principles and guidelines are needed to save this style of doing Christian ethics from expediency and lawlessness.

Is there any way to avoid the opposite ailments of the arthritis of legalism and the vertigo of lawlessness? The normative pattern here proposed would move beyond these two polar opposites, providing guidelines for the forms Christian love must take, as derived from the long Christian tradition of moral wisdom, yet also weighing seriously in the equation the changing circumstances that demand fresh translations of what love requires and flexibility of improvisation in relating love to the particulars of policy decision.

Between the Faith and the Facts

The model for doing Christian ethics in this technological culture, transcending legalism or lawlessness, is what could be called "double contextualism." There are two main frames or contexts within which Christian action takes place. One is the empirical context of the facts with the values at stake in them that constitute the circumstances enclosing choices. The other is the context of faith, the ultimate framework of theological and ethical norms, out of allegiance to which Christian action is motivated. Christian decision stands at the interface of these two contexts, between the "is" and the "ought," between the facts and the faith.

The initial obligation in responsible decision-making is to take full account of the *facts* that make up the limiting or permissive circumstances surrounding decision. At this first stage Christian ethics should hear all the factual information that science can provide about the "whats" and the "hows" of the natural and human world. On such a complex public problem as welfare reform or zoning laws or alternate sources of energy, or on such a private problem as parental discipline of children or premarital sex, wise decisions should be informed by as accurate and as full an acquaintance as possible with the hard facts of all sorts—geological, chemical, physiological, psychological, sociological, and the cause-effect sequences which the physical scientist or social scientist traces out. Obviously, it is impossible for anyone to know but a minuscule portion of the whole gamut of facts pertinent to such a matter as nuclear energy policy, for example. Even the skilled technicians will very likely disagree, and all sorts of sly and subtle biases color the interpretation and selection of facts. Furthermore, decisions have to be made today, long before all the relevant data can possibly be gathered in. Nonetheless, responsible choice must first assess as best it can what are the empirical facts.

Embedded in this welter of facts, as the second dimension of the proximate context, are the *values at stake*. An ethical decision, whether based on Christian or secular premises, is always difficult, sometimes agonizing, because it is never posed as a neat option between what is plainly good and what is plainly bad, but rather as a forced choice between two *goods*, or, it may be, between "the lesser of two evils." Life forecloses the possibility of having both goods, of "having one's cake and eating it too." Within a moral economy of scarcity, one value has to be sacrificed out of preference for another. All serious choices come to be in this sense compromises, where one is compelled to "rob Peter to pay Paul." Compromise means simply the sacrifice of one good out of allegiance to a preferred good, when the two conflict. To say that compromise is as inevitable as breathing is not to say that *all* compromises are equally good. For there are better and worse compromises. Yet the absolutely uncompromised life, as I have defined it, is not possible to live. That is why the preacher's hearty injunction "to serve all people" or "to love all" is of little help to a person or a nation in making domestic, vocational, political or foreign policy decisions, since the option posed is not between loving all people and hating them. The urgent question is: *which* persons or nations are to be served, when their interests or needs collide at the nexus of choice, and some have to be preferred over others?

There are at least three dimensions of the value-complex embedded in the circumstances of ethical choice. The first has to do with *what* values are at stake. Both in commonsense "conventional wisdom" and in moral philosophy there is a scale or hierarchy of values ranging from the "foundational" values, life itself, health, vitality, physical comforts, economic security, up through the social values of fellowship and friendship to the "higher" values of intellectual and aesthetic accomplishment. "Lower" and "higher" do not here mean morally bad *versus* morally good; rather, they mean foundational versus superstructural, or "instrumental" versus "intrinsic." While it is true that to be fully human involves the realization of the whole hierarchy of these personal values, the physical and social context of finitude and ambiguity often puts these values in collision as to ranking, and it becomes necessary to sacrifice on one to pursue another, as, for example when I sacrifice on sleep to meet a deadline for a writing project, or conversely, when I take a nap in class and miss all that intellectual wisdom voiced at the front end of the room.

The second dimension of the value-complex is the *time* dimension, where present assured values collide with possible future ones, where the good of the bird in the hand runs against that of two in the bush. "Look before you leap." "He who hesitates is lost." Which of these sayings is more true? Neither maxim is all-sufficient for moral choices, where capital risked on the future collides with present security. The customer is enjoined to "Buy now, pay later," but is *now* or *later* the most propitious time?

The third dimension of the value-complex, and the most crucial for Christian ethical reflection and action, is the *social* dimension: that is, *whose* values are at stake? Here the perennial clash is between "us" and "them" or, to put it more formally, between the self-interested concern for the protection of the goods of my family, neighborhood, race, class, nation as opposed to the other-interested concern for the different family, neighborhood, race, class, nation, "those over there." As we shall see, Christian ethics has much to say normatively about this problem: here it should only be underscored that prior to the ethical leap, one should not only look at the facts but sort out what and whose values stand in opposition in the context.

Yet even a clearheaded *de*scription of all the pertinent facts and of the values at stake (what is currently called "value clarification") does not of itself provide the moral *pre*scription for action. A moral "ought" cannot simply be derived from an empirical "is." To try to do so is to fall into the "naturalistic fallacy." All the empirical facts in the world about what is *desired* laid end to end would not lead to a moral conclusion about what is *desirable* or morally good. A Gallup poll of even the most careful and complete sort assessing ratios of public opinion on this or that does not determine that the majority is morally right, objectively speaking. Quantity of opinion does not assure quality of opinion. The crowd may be wrong. The norms of the good must come from somewhere else than the empirical context. The "naturalistic fallacy" is as dangerous on the one side as the "moralistic fallacy" is on the other: the notion that we should disregard the facts and circumstances and firmly or boldly do what's *right*, no matter what everybody's doing.

Here, incidentally, comes into view one of the dangerous by-products of the religion of scientism discussed in the first chapter. The magnificent achievements in technological research and the huge reservoir of power in technical know-how have led many to say, without much trouble of conscience, in the areas of genetic control or weaponry, for instance, that we *ought* to do the things we are technically capable of doing. From the Christian standpoint, the answer to this scientistic prescription is: "Wait. A prior question must be answered: What moral ends and purposes are to be served?" Technical know-how is not the supreme rule of conscience in Christian ethics. There are many things we are technically capable of doing that we should not do, out of allegiance to a God higher than the god of scientism, and to the humane goods his will requires.

For the "oughts," the moral norms and guidelines for decision, the Christian turns in the other direction: to the context of the Christian faith. This frame of faith also contains two levels within itself: the value-system normative for Christian living and the theological faith-premises which underlie and legitimate these moral goods, providing their ultimate sanction.

The Christian Conscience at the Crux of Decision

Before we examine what normative guidelines are derived from the context of the Christian faith, we must focus on the experience of the Christian as he or she stands precisely at the interface between the facts and the faith, or as someone phrased it, "with the Bible in one hand and the *New York Times* in the other." In the anatomy of Christian conscience there are many elements; the main ones can be summarized briefly. For one thing, the conscientious self is aware of its frailty and finitude, of its very limited reach of mind in its comprehension of reality and of the will in its scope of concern and in the range of moral maneuver open to it. The conscience also is aware of its sin, its biases and prejudices that have already prevented an "objective" reading of the facts and have twisted the data to suit its own self-interest. In other words, the conscience does not come to its decisions innocently, but already partial toward seeking and guarding its own provinces of power. As it stands under the judgment and grace of God, however, at the foot of the cross, the conscience of a Christian is made contrite. It is empowered by the forgiveness of grace to distance itself from its own partiality and is liberated from the tight circle of self-concern into a gracious and free life-style. Gracious living is thus a response to the forgiving grace of God.

Also, the Christian conscience has a measure of genuine freedom of choice, a freedom, to be sure, limited by the narrow confines of all the determining circumstances of the empirical context, yet a crucial freedom to choose the better over the worse and to alter thereby the circumstances of subsequent choices. This freedom is a "dreadful" freedom, in the sense that the self is *not* free *not* to choose; choice is required. Even *not* to choose is a form of choice. Nor is the self free from the inexorable consequences of choice; the fallout is of major moment. But it is also a glorious freedom, in that it is an endowment by the grace of God empowering a person to change the quality of life, inwardly and outwardly, insofar as the choice is made in obedience to the model of what God in Christ both gives and requires: obedient and faithful love.

Responsible Love

Here we come to the heart of the matter: the meaning of Christian love. The word "love" itself is used with so many different meanings—sexual attraction, cordiality, politeness, friendliness, pity, to name but a few—that it becomes difficult to detect its distinctive Christian meaning. In essence, as delineated in the New Testament, embodied in the person of Jesus Christ, and symbolized by the cross, Christian love (*agape* in the Greek) means a self-giving, uncalculating concern for the welfare of the neighbor, out of response to the manner of God's love to the human family. It is two-dimensional: "vertically," it is responsible *to* God; "horizontally," it is responsible *for* neighbor. To be accountable *to* God *for* the neighbor's well-being may entail, therefore, an obligation to distinguish what the neighbor really *needs* from what the neighbor *wants*. Discipline, restraint, withholding is often a needful expression of Christian love, as wise parents come to discover in dealing with their sometimes wayward children. But though love's way may require discipline, its ultimate purpose is gracious. Christian forgiveness reaches beyond restraint to reconciliation, after the fashion of God's forgiving grace that goes beyond judgment to reconcile and make new.

A second distinctive feature of Christian love lies in Christ's answer to the question: "But who is my neighbor?" The normal answer to that defines the neighbor as "one-of-my-own-kind." We should do good to those in our own family, town, nation, race, company. But such love is the friendship of like-for-like. Christian love, as defined in the parable of the good Samaritan, is radically different: it requires concern both for the like and the *un*like, as the Samaritan, the hated outlander with whom a good Jew would have no dealings, proved in being neighbor to the Jew who fell among thieves. This definition cuts through all the partial, selective, "fastidious," limited lines that persons draw in their range of concern, and opens out love's concern to universal neighborhood, just as God is not selective in his bounty, but " 'makes his sun rise on the evil and on the good, and sends rain on the just and on the unjust.' " The distant neighbor, the stranger, the enemy, the unlovable become the object of Christian concern.

Traditional Christian ethical theory has been mostly preoccupied with the psychology and theology of love. But there is another dimension, too, which currently is proving to be of vital concern: the ecological. The ethics of human relationship to the natural environment has been sharply debated both inside and outside the circle of Christian ethics. Some have claimed that God's injunction to Adam in Genesis to "subdue" the earth has proved a Christian warrant for the exploitation of nature which has brought us to our present perilous plight. Others have read Christianity as a kind of nature-mysticism, making all of nature divine and all levels of life to be equally revered. The more authentic reading of what Christian love requires in relation to nature is the ethics of stewardship: "The earth is the LORD's, and the fulness thereof." Like Adam, we are set in the world "to till it, and to keep it," to use it as faithful stewards. Fidelity in stewardship means to use nature out of service to neighbor in reverent love of God.

Justice: The Bridge Between Love and Public Policy

There yet remains a wide gap between the norm of love as so defined and the tangled morass of moral ambiguities and competing values that make up the context in which policy must be framed. In the traffic of business and politics, as well as in the more intimate circles of home and school, it is impossible to love all persons, and nature as well, with the same spontaneous grace that Christ's love in its pure form would require.

To bridge this gap, the norm of *justice* provides the way that love may be expressed in the world of systems and colliding values and needs. What should be the true interrelation of moral norms of justice and love has been an issue revived in recent discussion in the thought of Reinhold Niebuhr and many other ethicists who have been struggling to relate Christian love to public policy. Following Niebuhr's line of thought, we may say that justice is the oblique or indirect expression of love in those human decisions that affect many persons. The will to justice is here understood to mean not just a mechanical retribution, tit for tat, but a will to realize the highest possible quality of life for the widest possible range of persons.

The inner spirit of justice which infuses and changes the outer rules and laws by which the traffic of life goes on at home, in the courts, in the office, or on the playing field, can qualify as genuinely Christian when certain definable characteristics are present. For one: *fairness*. The administration of the rules is "fair" when those in power call the shots impartially, disinterestedly, without bias and prejudice bent to favor those calling the shots. The Christian ingredient in such fairness is precisely the non-self-interestedness of a love which "does not insist on its own way."

Another quality of justice is *equity*. "Equality under the law" has long been a moral norm of Anglo-Saxon jurisprudence, and the inspiration of civil rights legislation, for the protection of minorities, and for ERA in our own day. The same for all; the scales should be exactly even. The Christian will driving for such equality is the recognition of the common ground of creatureliness of all persons, and the obligation to the Creator to care for the neighbor as he or she stands there with the same basic needs and wants as all others in the human family.

But of course the human situation is never one where all neighbors confront the deciding self on a flat level par. Rather, the circumstances of choice press on the conscience a complex array of *un*equal merits, achievements, rights, needs, and wants. And there are the "rights" of the natural environment, too, that come into the crucible of decision, where often the protection of the land seems to conflict with the vitality of the economy. Just on the human level, every person is unique. Every case is different. In a sense, this means there is a lack of precedence in every judicial decision to be made, as well as precedence. To treat dissimilar cases similarly would be unjust. So, authentic justice must be *unequal* both in its retributions and distributions, or "proportional" to the variety of need and merit in the cases about which it must decide. It is here particularly that the spirit of Christian love tempers proportional justice. For from the Hebrew prophets to the present the Judeo-Christian conscience has asked that the scales of justice be tipped in favor of the poor, the dispossessed, the hungry, the needy, the weak. The justice and righteousness called for by Amos and Isaiah and Jesus as the only authentic worship of God were a recall of Israel to the terms of the covenant obligation with God, to make amends for the past injustices of the powerful who turned aside the needy at the gate and exploited the poor. In our own day, this prophetic ethic, to restore authentic community, gives the breaks to the deprived. It is this compassion which provides the moral logic, currently, for a steeply graded income tax, for "affirmative action" policies, for the Head Start program, federal low-cost housing projects—all the inequalities that advantage the disadvantaged and discriminate *for* those who have for so long been discriminated *against*.

Such a "reverse discrimination," as it is called, in the area of civil rights, for example, evokes angry protest from those formerly advantaged, the beneficiaries of scales long tipped the other way, and who now, by law, are disadvantaged (as in the Bakke case).

Withal, it is only realistic to acknowledge that no rules of justice in public policy can do full justice to what Christian love would require. For policy by definition is "class action," dealing with people in groups and blocs, by necessity treating persons as "cases" of this or that ethnic or economic category, as "Mexican" or "black." No proportional justice, however conscientious and refined, can fully love all neighbors as Christ loved us or be fully sensitive to the whole gamut of individual needs and merits. At best, then, public policy can only do "rough" justice to what *agape* would require. Though there remains always a tension, a distance, between justice and love, justice as tempered by mercy stands as the normative guideline for Christian social witness and action. To seek such a relative rough justice is the absolute Christian imperative.

3

Matters of
Life and Death

> Science has made gods of us before we have deserved to
> be men.
>
> *Jean Rostand*

Currently one of the most troubled arenas of moral decision is that of medical ethics. At first glance it would seem that the questions about the right or wrong of contraception, abortion, euthanasia, genetic control, recombinant DNA, etc. are matters of law and public policy, to be left to the technical experts to decide, certainly not to laity. But in fact they are also decisions of the most intimate and private sort for individuals, life-and-death matters indeed. The often cruel dilemmas posed by them are not solved by saying, "Leave it to the doctors to decide. Or the courts. They know what's right to do." To be sure, doctors may have the technical knowledge of "how," but the ethical question of "whether," technique itself cannot answer, as leaders in the medical profession usually are the first to acknowledge. And the laws of the courts are not fixed, but sustained or changed by the tugs and turns of public convictions about morality. Where then *is* the Supreme Court of *moral* authority?

It is common knowledge that rapid progress in medical science has increased enormously human control over life-making, life-sustaining, and life-taking processes. Whereas, by the conventional wisdom of the past, Providence or nature was usually assumed to have command over birth and death ("Most merciful Father, who hast been pleased to take unto thyself the soul of this thy servant . . ."), now these matters increasingly fall into the hands of humans who are forced to play God whether they want to or not. Not entirely, of course. There are fixed limits and constants of the human condition that are not altered by technology: death is inevitable, however later than sooner it has been postponed by medical science. As sexual passion and the mating habit are perennial, so too are the abiding constants of human loves and hates, sympathies and antipathies, estrangements and reconciliations that make up the human story between birth and death. "Sibling rivalry" goes back at least as far as Cain and Abel, and marital love as well as dissension presumably to Adam and Eve.

Lest we think that the free expression of sexuality is a phenomenon unique to the twentieth century, it is well to remember the old rhyme:

> King David and King Solomon
>   Led merry, merry lives,
> With many, many lady friends
>   And many, many wives;
> But then old age crept over them—
>   With many, many qualms,
> King Solomon wrote the Proverbs,
>   And King David wrote the Psalms.

Our concern here is not with these constants but with the variables, with the changed circumstances for human choice which are the consequences of applied scientific research and have now posed challenges to traditional ethical standards and the laws that reflect them. To give some system to my approach to these problems, I will make use of the model of "double contextualism" outlined in the previous chapter.

Making Love and Making Babies

First, the empirical facts. Though all sorts of crude contraceptive devices and practices have been used for centuries, it has been only in this century that medical research has perfected artificial contraceptives that are quite safe and sure, although lately there is mounting evidence of health hazards in even such a widely used contraceptive as "the Pill," earlier presumed to be completely safe.

Contraceptives are readily available, even "across the counter." One might expect that this would contribute to the increased frequency of sexual relations among the unmarried, especially teenagers. There is no sure way to know if non-marital sexual relations using contraceptives have increased. They probably have; in any case it is certain that teenage sexual relations have increased, as witness the phenomenal rise in teenage pregnancies in the last decade.

There are other cultural factors, some only indirectly the consequences of the technological revolution, that are at work here. The span of years is getting longer between the time of sexual maturity (about 13 or 14 for girls) and the time when a young couple have finished school and are in an economic position to get married and start a home of their own. Add to this the worship of Aphrodite in the sacraments of advertising, titillating the senses with appeals and promises that sexual attraction is the true bond of love and mutual orgasm the height of human happiness. No surprise, then, that in the context of the unchaperoned, cozy collegiate existence of coed dorms there is such a high incidence of casual and relatively guiltless sexual relations. The traditional Christian moral legalism that reserved intercourse for the monogamous family relation seems rather tacky. Moreover, in popular Freudian terms, Christian prohibitions are repressive of what is natural and good. Why not enjoy sex when you can and with whomever, since, thanks to technology, nobody gets hurt?

There are several values that collide at the point of decision in the conscience of any sensitive young person in the sex-saturated culture we have described. The freedom to sleep with one's lover, or for a couple to live together on a trial basis, an informal arrangement which can be canceled when either party "wants out," runs smack against the values of security and stability in a permanent marriage relationship, blessed and sanctioned by church and state, when each partner takes a vow of permanent fidelity each to the other "for better, for worse," a binding obligation for the whole way.

A value conflict of a very different sort created by technological improvements in contraceptive methods appears in the debate about birth control for anybody, married or unmarried. On a worldwide basis, the population explosion, or the "population bomb" as Paul Ehrlich called it, has made demographers aware that the human species is itself endangered if the rate of population increases at its present exponential pace. The world's population reached three billion in 1960. With the much-extended lifespan and the lowered infant mortality rate which health sciences have produced, the world's population is expected to reach 7.2 billion by the year 2000, when there will be two persons standing where one now stands. In light of the depletion of the earth's resources to sustain life, even the "green revolution" which is the application of technology in agriculture, greatly increasing the yield of the soil, will not stave off an unintended mass genocide by starvation.

To be sure, the problem is more ominous in the underdeveloped nations than in the overdeveloped nations like the United States, where the rate of population growth is now nearly zero; but the value conflict is acute everywhere. Essentially, it is the collision between quantity of life and quality of life. That is, presuming an economy of scarcity, a smaller quantity of children may enjoy a higher quality of life in terms of nutrition and educational opportunity, whereas the family with six or eight children in a rural or city slum will be deprived both of lower and higher values, simply because there is not enough to go around. The temporal dimension of the value conflict is apparent too: adequate resources for the present generation are pitched against the needs of posterity. Therefore to limit the birth rate drastically would seem an imperative for everyone. But it is not quite that simple. There is not always an exactly inverse ratio between density of the mass and the quality of humane living. Given a certain adequate economic base, there are spiritual and psychological values in the give-and-take among a sizable number of children, and rich personal blessings for their parents, which are unavailable to the only child or childless couple. And one of the reasons for the resistance to birth control among the impoverished of the world is the strong spiritual need of parents for the security which they feel may be provided for them by their children when they become old and feeble. This is a qualitative factor that weighs against the quantitative consideration of having not enough food and too many mouths to feed when the children are young.

The Relevance of Responsible Love

To make responsible decisions amid this tangle of perilous sociological facts and competing values poses hard problems for the Chris-

tian conscience. For the teenager, in college or not, confronted by
the free and easy sexual practices of his or her peers, "in love" or not,
what guidance might be found in Christian ethics?

Despite the popular stereotype that Christian means "puritan,"
viewing sexuality with suspicion ("God's one mistake in creation,"
one frustrated monk put it), a normative Christian position is that
sexuality, as part of the good order of creation, is a relational good;
that is, it finds its true value within a context of certain psychological
or spiritual relations. The sexual act of intercourse in a physiological
sense is not *per se* love. What makes it an expression of love, rather
than of lust, is a spiritual matter, the terms of personal relation that
obtain between the two persons involved. In the Greek, the three
different words *eros, philia,* and *agape* convey crucial distinctions
that the English word "love" obscures. Love as *eros* (or libido, to use
a Freudian term) means physical passion. *Philia* means companionship, mutual delight in shared tastes, tasks, and recreations. *Agape*
means long-range commitment, fidelity, tenderness, sacrificial concern for the well-being of the other. The true bonds of a lasting marriage are *philia* and *agape.* This does not mean that *eros* is wrong,
that a Christian marriage is physically passionless. It means rather
that sex finds its true worth and meaning when set within the context
of the shared tasks, joys, and worries of making a home, and in the
one-with-one bond of exclusive fidelity: the monogamous family unit.
Physiologically the act of sexual intercourse a man has with a prosti-
tute might be the same experience as intercourse with his wife. The
difference is a spiritual one, different terms of relationship in which
the sex act takes place. When libido is "agapaic," seeking the satisfaction of the other, it is love; when libido "uses" another for self-
satisfaction, it is lust. To acknowledge that within legally formalized
marriages there is often exploitation and lust, and that agapaic love
may be present before the bonds of marriage are publicly, legally
tied, does not cancel the normative point: by and large sex finds its
true moral worth within the one-with-one bond of monogamous marriage. This Christian understanding of the relation of sex to love provides a moral compass point from which to move into the ambiguities
of choice. Sexual intimacy proportional to the degree of permanence
and long-term fidelity becomes right and good. And permanence and

long-term fidelity are cultivated out of personal affinities and sympathies more than physical passion.

A fine but important three-way distinction needs to be made between non-marital, extra-marital, and pre-marital relations. By the criterion just set, *non*-marital relations, the kind of casual "sleeping around," done just for kicks, are morally wrong, even though by collegiate sophisticates they are not condemned as once they were. By the same token, *extra*-marital relations, breaking the vow of one-with-one fidelity, introduce the green jealousies and tensions of rivalry with the other man or the other woman—they too are wrong. As to *pre*-marital sexual relations, the situation is morally more complex. Suppose an engaged couple are compelled by educational or economic circumstances to postpone their formal marriage and home-making. Since they strongly feel that in spirit they are pledged to each other in marriage, they may feel that they could have full sexual relations with no sense of guilt. There are risks, yes, for circumstances and affections may change, but then nothing in life is riskless. The complexities of this risk, however, may turn out to be far more involved and difficult than they had imagined.

The answers to the larger question of birth control and planned parenthood are more visible. There is, to be sure, a division in the Christian church between the official Roman Catholic doctrine on the one hand which proscribes all *artificial* modes of contraception (though "natural" methods are legitimate), on the premise that such interfere with the divine intention of sexuality: procreation, and Protestant church leaders and ethicists, on the other, who generally approve all of the artificial contraceptive devices perfected by medical science and encourage their use and the spread of information about them. The Roman Catholic position, fitted to an early or medieval culture, does not really face up to the consequences of the population explosion and is rendered obsolete by technological developments. In fact, it is not even practiced by a majority of the devout, at least in North America. Under the dark threat of the population explosion, and with the decreasing resources of the earth, it becomes a Christian imperative to turn the line of the population curve down, if possible, to increase the chances for a higher quality of life for the fewer persons. Through education and birth-control clinics, especially in economically depressed areas at home and abroad, medical technology can become the ally of Christian justice.

The Abortion Debate

The rate of teenage child-bearing in the United States is one of the highest in the world. Two-thirds of the one million teenage pregnancies each year are unintentional and over half of these young pregnant women are unmarried. Of the total number of teenage pregnancies approximately 600,000 result in births.[1]

This is but one bit of evidence to show that despite the wide availability of contraceptives, the incidence of pregnancies, wanted or unwanted, is high, and of abortions, legal or illegal, on the increase.[2] The problem of the morality of abortion, underlying the debate about its legality, has prompted much heart-searching and fervent debate between those who favor and those who oppose it, for the value collisions are not as readily resolved as with the contraceptive issue, although both practices have the same intention: to prevent birth. (Is the use of the "morning-after" pill or IUD an act of contraception or abortion?)

Where medical technology weighs into the scales of moral choice is in the plain fact that abortions can now be performed with little or no risk to the life of the pregnant woman. The "kitchen-table-and-icepick" method of abortion is no longer necessary. Sophisticated techniques such as amniocentesis can detect some serious deformities in the fetus even in midpregnancy. Should a fetus be allowed to be brought to birth if its deformity is so serious that its existence could hardly be called "human"? Sometimes the health or very life of the mother may be at stake if the fetus should be brought to term. An infant born as a result of a conception by rape or incest, though such cases are comparatively rare, may be healthy physically, but the circumstances and home environment exceedingly unhealthy. Perhaps better, for his or her sake, that the child never had been born.

The more agonizing problems of conscience and policy arise in situations where there may be no serious medical problem, but where the social and psychological context of birth would forebode dark prospects for the life of the infant. A child born to an unmarried girl of fifteen who is totally unprepared for the tasks of motherhood, who lacks any family resources, or money, or support from the father of the infant, is up against formidable obstacles indeed. What should an ethics of caring do in such cases—of which there are hundreds of thousands each year?

The value conflicts in this empirical context are quite evident. It is life against life. If, as Roman Catholic doctrine affirms in such a papal encyclical as *Casti Connubii* (1930), the unborn fetus becomes a living soul at the time of "quickening," then to take the life of that person is indeed the "murder of the innocent." But this right to life of the unborn fetus clashes with the rights of the mother's life and health. Even conservative abortion opponents acknowledge that in such a clash of life with life, a therapeutic abortion to save the mother's life is justified.

But the more frequent value clashes arise in non-therapeutic abortion cases, between quantity and quality of life, where the questions of "whats" and "whose" are intermixed. There are many cases where conserving the life of a severely retarded infant, a mongoloid baby, for example, would spell murder for that child's parents in a spiritual and economic sense. And the cost to the supporting society, in medical expenses, would far outweigh the benefit which that child, if it should grow to maturity, might possibly contribute. But there is a graded continuum here between severe and slight retardation. No clear dividing line can be drawn by which to decide that aborting a fetus on one side of the line is right and on the other wrong. And though the emotional drain for parents raising a retarded child is severe, there are, as many such parents testify, spiritual benefits derived from their sustained care, as they learn to live by the ethics of the cross, the symbol of sacrificial and suffering love.

From the standpoint of the moral norm of Christian justice, as the indirect expression of responsible love, the landmark decision of the Supreme Court (Roe v. Wade, 1973) seems to balance these competing values well. The court affirmed that

> For the stage prior to approximately the end of the first trimester [3 months], the abortion decision and its effectuation must be left to the medical judgment of the pregnant woman's attending physician. . . .

> For the stage subsequent to . . . the end of the first trimester, the State, in promoting its interests in the health of the mother, may, if it chooses, regulate the abortion procedure in ways that are reasonably related to maternal health. . . .
>
> [During the last ten weeks of pregnancy, however, when the fetus is considered viable] the State, in promoting its interest in the potentiality of human life, may if it chooses, regulate, and even proscribe, abortion except where it is necessary, in appropriate medical judgment, for the preservation of the life or health of the mother.[3]

This is a permissive and compromised ruling, satisfying neither militant proponents nor opponents of abortion. In 1977 the Supreme Court qualified somewhat the liberal terms of its earlier ruling by declaring that states are not required to use public funds such as Medicaid to offer elective, non-therapeutic abortions for free. But the moral logic of the 1973 decision is that as the fetus comes nearer and nearer to term, the moral center of gravity shifts from the rights of the mother and her physician to the right to life of the fetus.

Any public policy should attempt to do the best possible proximate justice to the ultimate Christian norm of love. The value of life should be measured not only quantitatively but qualitatively. A "Call to Concern," signed by many Christian theologians and ethicists put the matter well: "Considering the best medical advice, the best moral insight, and a concern for the total quality of the whole life cycle for the born and the unborn, we believe that abortion may in some instances be the most loving act possible."[4]

The Right to Die

Early in 1976, the Karen Quinlan case brought to public notice in a dramatic and poignant way another point where medical technology poses novel ethical problems and a cruel choice. Here was a girl whose cerebral damage from alcohol and possibly drugs had rendered her for months comatose, suffering "brain death," totally unresponsive to stimuli, yet by an artificial respirator and other devices kept "alive." Her Roman Catholic parents, with the blessing of their priest, pleaded in the courts for her to be allowed to die with dignity. The New Jersey court decision denied their request. Even after the respirator was removed, Karen Quinlan was kept "breathing" and "alive" for a long time by artificial life-prolonging (some would call them "death-prolonging") procedures, but as a vegetable, dead to the world. Was the court decision morally right, or should her parents' request have been granted?

In much less poignant and news-making ways than in Karen Quinlan's case, technology has created a new context of circumstances where life-or-death decisions are posed as for no previous generation. A century ago the average expected lifespan for an American was about 40 years. Now it is about 70, thanks to preventive medicine, health care, improved housing, sanitation, and nutrition, and many surgical and medical breakthroughs such as organ transplants. It is now possible by artificial respirators, intravenous feedings, etc., to extend life in a biological sense long after life in any normal sense has gone, when responses to stimuli are lacking, when the patient is but a breathing corpse, and a medical prognosis gives no hope of recovery.

Here again, as with the abortion problem, the values in collision are between life in a quantitative sense and life in a qualitative sense. The Hippocratic oath obliges the doctor to prolong life and "help the sick, . . . to do no injury or wrongdoing." But should he or she prolong life by any and every technical means? Yet who can define life or clock the precise moment of death, for that matter? Death is a gradual process of stages: clinical death, brain death, biological death, cellular death. And long before these physical stages of death are reached, life in a spiritual sense may no longer be worth living. In such cases, should not the right to die be honored?

Another value conflict is in the cost-benefit equation: what are the benefits to keeping a patient alive, when the costs to that patient's family and to society, in attempting a kidney transplant for example, are exorbitant? Preserve life at any cost? But in an economy of scarcity, might not the expense for a single kidney transplant be more justly spent on preventive medical care for the health clinic in India, where the lives of hundreds of children might be saved?

There is one distinctive mind-set of modern culture that colors the debate about the morality and the legality of euthanasia. In previous cultures of the West, where Christian faith set the frame of thought about living and dying, this life was regarded as a brief and transient pilgrimage to another life beyond this "vale of tears." In contrast, our post-Christian culture, generally uncertain about life after death, tends to view this life as the only sure one. Therefore death is feared as the great Enemy, to be put off as long as possible by whatever means. Morticians often capitalize on this fear of death, using cosmetics to make the corpse appear "lifelike." The fear of death as enemy collides with the desire to say *"Komm, süsser Tod,"* and embrace death as friend and blessing.

The dominant motif in a normative Christian ethical policy to be brought to bear on every decision for or against euthanasia is a care for persons, prior over even the care for biological life itself. In the face of illness, even of a severe sort, where there are the resources at hand and a prognosis of a likely or possible recovery, Christian morality would certainly expect and require all the skills of therapy that technology can provide. When, on the other hand, the situation is deemed hopeless, and meaningful responsive personal existence for the patient has ended, where suffering is acute and prolonged, it is an act of Christian mercy (and that, of course, is literally what "euthanasia" means) to allow the patient to die with dignity, to liberate him or her from the shackles of pain. To allow the patient to die, by removing extraordinary life-support devices, is "passive" euthanasia. There may be a fine line between "passive" euthanasia and "active" euthanasia, where positive measures are taken, such as an injection of morphine or an overdose of pills, since the intent to cause death is the same, but the moral preference should be for "passive" euthanasia, to let nature take its benevolent course.

The willing consent of the patient should be presumed here. In many cases, however, that may not be possible. The condition of many elderly ill patients, under sedation and semiconscious, may prevent their rational decision to withhold or cease extraordinary measures to prolong their life. The decision may fall into the hands of their families, in consultation with the doctors attending. Where the family is involved, one may expect an agonizing tussle between mind and heart, between acknowledging, in the abstract, that euthanasia is the loving thing to do and the surging emotions one might feel in consenting that the life of a near and dear one should be taken, and subsequently a sense of guilt. Here the reassurance of the physician, or pastor or hospital chaplain, that the withdrawal of extraordinary measures is proper and legal would be an expression of personal concern. In all of such circumstances, however dreadful, the Christian moral norm holds good: the concern for persons. Prior to such dire extremities, and increasing number of people out of Christian concern frame a "Living Will," certifying the physical conditions under which they would wish that no artificial or heroic medical measures be applied to prolong their life unduly.

I have limited my discussions to those life-and-death issues where individual decisions have to be made, with or without the benefit of the technical experts. There are now emerging many new developments in medical research that increase even more human controls over life-making and life-sustaining processes, with radical changes no one can now foretell. Some hold great promise for human healing, to restore sight to the blind and hearing to the deaf, to cure cancer and other dread diseases. There are some areas of research whose consequences may bode as much ill as good, and where the risks of misuse are high. Extended research in DNA, cloning, genetic engineering, selective breeding, behavior control by drugs—all these already begin to pose momentous problems in bio-ethics with which persons of humane conscience must wrestle. But for now, since these scientific developments are still largely at the level of research, I leave their consideration to move on to other moral dilemmas of everyday living that arise in the fragile and fleeting span of the meanwhile between birth and death.

4

Work and Vocation

Laborare est orare (to labor is to pray)

No sector of human life has been more profoundly changed by the technological revolution than *work*, the human expenditure of energy to gain a livelihood in the production, distribution, and consumption of goods and services. The transformation of work-life by the wheel, the symbol of rational technique, has taken place both in direct ways that are highly visible and in more indirect ways that have produced the industrial, mechanical culture of the modern city. Whether directly or indirectly, our value-system or, if you like, our "character" or "soul," has been altered in ways that put the citizen of the twentieth century in a context so different from that of Biblical times as to render communication of wisdom from the Bible to industrial culture almost impossible.

The psalmist asks that God establish "the work of our hands." The work done in pre-industrial cultures was literally that: handwork, or work using the most primitive tools. But in this technocratic age, work is automated: the machine has almost completely displaced the hand. The mode of work also has shifted from agricultural to industrial and this within quite recent time. About one hundred and fifty years ago, 90% of Americans were engaged in agriculture; now, 6%. And even on the farm, the work is done by machine: the tractor has replaced the hoe.

By technique, in the discussion that follows, I mean not only the use of "hard" machinery, the tractor or the internal combustion engine, but the use of rational systems of interpersonal relations in the plant or the law office, in business and office management, in public administration, where complex "machineries" are used to achieve maximum efficiency in the vast bureaucracies of both the public and private sectors of common life.

By virtue of the character of the economy in industrial and professional and agricultural work, although people still talk fervently about "free enterprise" and individualism, you would have to look long and far to find a worker who is truly his or her own boss. Most persons work in and for some structured system, a huge corporation, or university, or factory plant, or bureaucracy, with little or no power or say-so about the policies and circumstances of their work or the rules of the game.

Within these systems at the office, or plant, or agency, technology requires a high degree of specialization of work. In the Ford plant, the industrial worker performs one minute operation over and over again as the parts move with relentless speed along the assembly line. In housebuilding, the "jack of all trades," the handyman, has disappeared; in his place appears the baseboard-heating installer who like as not does not know the first thing about shingling a roof. In medicine, the ophthalmologist is not trained to cope with a case of neuritis. In medicine, the specialist prevails; the general practitioner is a rare and endangered species.

In the rural economy of a century ago, work was done along a very short chain of links between the production and the consumption of food. Individual farmers saw the whole process through from their own seed to their own supper table. Now, the links of the chain are enormously extended and complex. Fertilization, cultivation, harvesting, transportation, packaging, wholesaling, retailing, purchasing —many different links are involved along this assembly line, not only for the simple necessities of food, clothing, and shelter, but for all the other goods and services of our economy. To the extent that a person *does* have a hand in the process, the scope of responsibility for each worker is limited to one tiny link. It is impossible to have a sense of the whole. The word for it is "fragmentation."

The *indirect* impacts of technology upon work-life are less plainly visible but no less profound. For one thing, the machine has moved people from the country to the city. Urbanization followed inevitably upon the Industrial Revolution, for the mechanical production of goods required factories and a concentration of population nearby.

Then housing, goods, and services grew up around the industrial center and a tangled cluster of schools, stores, and banks. As it sprawled further out, systems of transportation from home to job were needed. This in turn affected the life-style and ethos of the American family: nowadays, the father, if he is the major wage earner, goes from home "to work," to the plant, or the mine, or the laboratory, or the office. His home-life is divided from his work-life, and may split even his inner self in two. Peter Berger, in studying the sociology of work, notes this split:

> in an industrial society . . . people do not work where they carry on their private lives. The two spheres are geographically and socially separate. . . . one can say . . . that they do not live where they work. . . . Life at work thus tends to take on the character of pseudo-reality and pseudo-identity: "I only work here, but if you want to know me as I really am, come to my home and meet my family."[1]

The dynamics of the industrial machine-run economy seem to require that the GNP curve be constantly on the rise, that more and more goods be consumed and at a rapid rate of turnover, that the standard of living, as measured in quantity, be ever on the increase. This in turn may require that mother as well as father go to work, sometimes out of necessity, to make ends meet, sometimes out of a sense of worth, to put her advanced professional education to better use than in the wasteland and dross of housework, sometimes both. According to the Bureau of Labor Statistics, *both* parents in a majority of American families currently are employed outside the home, at least part-time, and the percentage of parents with full-time jobs steadily increases. This trend has mixed moral consequences: her self-fulfillment and liberation, but at the price of an unstabilizing impact upon family solidarity. Increasingly, despite sentimental talk and yearnings for hearth and home (and the curious persistent desire of people to have a fireplace in their new house, though functionally it is generally useless), home is the place you go through on the way to somewhere else. It is no longer, as it was a century ago, the heart's final destination.

A further consequence for family life-style of our urbanized, industrial economy is high mobility. One family out of about five or six in America moves every year. Americans purchase over 500,000 new mobile homes annually. Though in fact most people park and stay put in their mobile homes, there is a certain sales appeal in the very term "mobile." This mobility results in part from and contributes to a lack of roots in place or tradition or family heritage.

The Values at Stake

One might cite many other ways in which the machine, in taking work out of human hands, has changed drastically the human heart and self-image. Our interest here, though, is in sorting out the values at stake in this aspect of the technological revolution. What are the moral benefits and costs, the losses and gains for the human spirit, and what values are on a collision course?

The machine has emancipated us from the dreadful, life-killing drudgery to which for centuries people were enslaved. Compare the costs to human life and health of the way in which the pyramids of Egypt were built or the Great Wall of China, and the giant tombs of Emperor Chin Shih Huong Ti, in the second century B.C., with the way in which a New York City skyscraper is constructed, or Apollo 11. The score is surely a strong plus for the human benefits of technology. The tractor, and bulldozer, and all the techniques of the green revolution, have freed the farmer from the enslavement of Edwin Markham's "Man with the Hoe,"

> Bowed by the weight of centuries he leans
> Upon his hoe and gazes on the ground,
> The emptiness of ages in his face,
> And on his back the burden of the world.

Lest "urban nausea" lead one to harbor any illusions about the "good old days," think of the dreary and backbreaking round of menial chores, dawn to dusk, that enslaved Grandmother. By the electric this-or-that, in cooking, cleaning, washing, all members of the family are now freed for creative uses of time. The quick efficiency of the machine, replacing the slow work of the hand, is clearly the friend of the human spirit. It has made life more safe, convenient, and healthy, and has enriched immeasurably the opportunity for aesthetic, athletic, and intellectual pursuits.

But while in one sense technology has proved liberator, it also has brought a new form of tyranny and enslavement, the spiritual drudgery of assembly-line work, whether at the desk or at the factory, at home or on the road. At the textile plant, industrial workers are locked into the giant machinery, hardly more than cogs in the machine, and always threatened by the awareness that they could easily be displaced tomorrow by other cogs. In professional work, where one might expect greater latitude for personal initiative, workers are equally locked in by the system, by "roles" each one must play. It is not strange that the sign TGIF ("Thank God It's Friday") appears often on the secretary's desk, or in the secretary's mind, promising at least weekend parole from the prison of the office routine.

Another subtle form of tyranny by technology appears in consumerism, the onslaught of commercial advertising badgering the housewife with the nostrums of the doctrine of salvation by gadgetry, wheedling, seducing, even commanding her to go to her nearest shopping center tomorrow to purchase the newest electromatic this-or-that. If she does not, it is implied, she will have to stumble along in the dark night of inefficiency. Never mind about the cost. "Buy now, pay later." The tyranny of gadgetry is as cruel in its way, especially for people of low income, as the tyranny of menial housework was for those who lacked the sophisticated devices that crowd the modern kitchen.

Another value collision present in the mechanization of work is between the pragmatic value of efficiency as it conflicts with the worth of the persons involved. In the office, or factory, there may be an inverse ratio between efficiency in output and sensitivity to personal needs. The machine reduces the opportunity for personal initiative, imagination, daring, courage, heroism. Why are there so few heroes or heroines on the horizon? Even in one of the boldest ventures of the twentieth century, the exploration of outer space, the astronauts are relatively anonymous, with nothing like the renown of a Columbus, a Magellan, a Peary, or a Lindbergh, simply because the instruments in the Houston Control Center make the crucial decisions for them. The spaceship itself masterminds and guides them, not they it. The machine is the hero of the piece.

The term that appears most commonly in the studies of work in America is the word "alienation." It means, of course, estrangement, or a rupture in the sense of personal involvement.

Our technological work-life is alienated in a double sense. For one, the machine intercepts between the worker and whatever he or she works at, reducing the sense of personal involvement, creativity, imagination, craft, and skill. In another sense, the fragmentation of work reduces both the sense of wholeness in seeing the job through from beginning to end, and also the sense of accountability, for the worker can never see or know the one who consumes what he or she works at or, for that matter, few if any of the others in the complex chain of production. Shoddy work is one consequence of this. ("They don't make things the way they used to.") Obsolescence is another. That things wear out faster may not seem to be a mark of their efficiency, but in another sense it is an economically efficient policy, assuring as it does the rapid turnover of goods to keep the GNP line on the rise. One factor in this devil's brew is the assumption that work of any kind is morally right, idleness sinful. So "made" work is needed—no matter what is produced—to keep the GNP moving up.

As an important HEW study of *Work in America* documents, monotonous tasks and dreary regimentation are common to both factory and office, to men and women, to black and white, and the cost to employees—and the nation—may be huge. These costs in worker alienation, alcoholism, drug addiction and other symptoms of poor mental health derive from our national policies and attitudes toward work.[2] Efficiency, the supreme moral good of technology, thus collides with the value of the dignity and worth of persons, the supreme moral good of Judeo-Christian ethics.

In sum, alienation means that what I work *at* is split from what I work *for*. What I work *at* has to do with the external action of my hands and head, but since personal involvement is cut off by the machine or the system, what I work *for*, that is, the motives of my heart, are extraneous to the operation itself. My heart is in securing benefits and satisfactions like better wages, fewer hours, better peer-group relations, etc. All sorts of studies of industrial work confirm the conclusions of Elton Mayo made years ago that workers consider the social function of the enterprise the most important. The major demands of industrial workers appear as demands for good and close group relationships with their fellow workers, for good relations with supervisors, for advancement, and above all for recognition as human beings, for social prestige satisfactions, for status and function.[3]

Christian Vocation and Technical Work

In this tangled work-world, with all the moral ambiguities that the machine has brought into human work-life, no wonder that the ancient Christian norms seem irrelevant. Remote indeed sound the words of Brother Lawrence, a monk of the seventeenth century whose worship and work were of a piece:

> "The time of business . . . does not with me differ from the time of prayer, and in the noise and clatter of my kitchen, while several persons are at the same time calling for different things, I possess God in as great tranquillity as if I were upon my knees at the blessed sacrament."[4]

That the work of our hands should be done for the glory of God and the service of neighbor, that labor should be a form of prayer, are norms very distant from a personnel-management decision about break-times in the night-shift schedule at the steel plant. If a preacher should invade the G.M. plant, and shout to those on the night shift, *"Laborare est orare"* ("to labor is to pray")—assuming anyone could hear over the racket—the response would likely be quite irreverent, if not profane.

So great is the distance between the ethics of the cross, of sacrificial Christian love, and the ethics of the wheel, of tight rational technical efficiency, that it is not surprising that commonly our culture copes with the distance by a complete split between Sunday worship and weekday work. Or alternatively by another split between those engaged in "Christian" work, i. e., the clergy, and those in secular work, the laity, who must operate by different moral rules. In a study of the ethics of one business executive, Kenneth Underwood describes the difficulties and tensions any responsible business executive would feel who might try to be Christian in work. Said one such executive, " 'I much more easily identify myself with Pontius Pilate, and the problems he faced, than with Jesus Christ.' "[5]

Yet look again. There is an indirect but rich relevance of the Christian doctrine of vocation to technological work. Martin Luther restated the Biblical norm of vocation in a telling fashion. He protested the medieval two-story division of labor between those on the upper floor of the house of faith, who did "religious" work, the monk or nun, and those on the lower floor who did "secular" work, the merchant or carpenter or farmer or magistrate. No, said Luther, all believers are called by God to serve their neighbors in love, out of gratitude for the gift of grace in Christ. All believers in this sense are priests; all should be "Christs" to their neighbors. *Vocatio* means that one is called by God and accountable to God for the well-being of the neighbor. The motivation *for* work, then, was religious: to show forth the praise of God in the work of one's hands, in whatever line, to maintain the fabric of community.

In Luther's culture of small town and farm, the context was one where that accountability was closely checked, for the carpenter knew personally the family down the road for whom he was caning a chair or making a chest of drawers. Integrity and care in one's craft were more likely to ensue from such a combination of inner motive and outer circumstance. The sense of vocation unified what one worked *at* with what one worked *for*. And workers were more likely to be called to account for the quality of their products by a neighbor they knew than by customers they would never know.

Though it is a great cultural distance between Luther's carpenter in Wittenberg and the office on the fortieth floor of a Manhattan skyscraper, there *are* some ways in which it is possible to revise economic policies and practices in such a way as to restore meaning in work and realize something of what vocation signifies. The hope and promise for such changes rests on the premise, implicit throughout this book, that we need not be the victim of our machines, like the children of Frankenstein, but can make them instruments of humane purposes.

One important study of the problem of work summarizes the main elements in the syndrome of work-satisfaction as follows: (1) creating something, (2) using skill, (3) working wholeheartedly, (4) using initiative and having responsibility, (5) mixing with people, and (6) working with people who know their job.[6]

Recovery from the dreary monotony and empty meaninglessness of industrial as much as professional work lies through regard for the whole person of the worker as of prior importance to the function he or she performs. In business management and personnel policies there are many kinds of programs—more serious than the office cocktail party at Christmas—that give explicit form to this concern for the whole person: job redesign, job rotation, retraining for a variety of jobs. Team-work projects, now used in some automobile plants, where a team of persons will be responsible for the whole assembly process, both overcome the fragmentation and monotony of the assembly-line method, as HEW studies have documented, and improve the quality of the products as well. In the professional business world, policies of "flexitime" provide release from the prison of the 9-to-5 schedule, and actually increase rather than decrease productivity as well as personal satisfaction in the job. There is a mixture of motives here where businesses or industries initiate these personnel policies, increased efficiency and productivity among them. But one motive present in the mix, consciously or unconsciously, is a Christian intent: a concern for the sacred worth of persons, to be realized through opening ways to exercise imagination, creativity, and responsibility.

Another form through which the Christian meaning of vocation can be restored is through restructuring power so as to give the worker a voice in determining the policies and conditions under which he or she works. For the large part, in the capitalist economy of America, this originally was and still remains a central moral purpose propelling the labor union movement. The regard for the worker as a person, not just as one of the "hands" in the textile plant, is an expression of Christian love translated into social justice. The labor contract, determining hours and wage rate, grievance procedures, retirement benefits, etc., may seem to be entirely economic and mercenary, but the invisible bottom line of the contract negotiated and followed, or of a strike threatened or called, is the moral issue of justice in the distribution of power. Such humanizing purposes are not the monopoly of the trade union movement alone, to be sure. In fact, in these latter days, many policies of "big" labor have proven as dehumanizing in their way as the corruptions of the older monopolies of power they first were intended to offset. Personnel policies in business or governmental or university administrations, even where there is no union, may also have a democratic power structure and reflect a concern for persons and the justice that encourages both cooperation and protest from all parties. Where management and labor, unionized or not, combine their varied skills in viewing the process of production as a whole, so that one worker learns the indispensability of the other, meaning in the work of each is restored, and something of the original spirit of Christian vocation is recovered.

Housekeeping and Homemaking

One of the calls trumpeted in the women's liberation movement is for escape from the stark, lonely prison of housekeeping. The gap in the ratio of women to men with college and advanced degrees is slowly closing. With all their professional skills, it is manifestly an injustice perpetuated by male chauvinists that their abilities should be frustrated by their being confined to quarters, to housekeeping and baby-tending. Or such is the cry of protest. By any criterion of Christian humanitarian justice, it *is* surely wrong that a woman working full-time earns on the average some 60% of what a man earns in a job of comparable quality. "Affirmative action" policies in hiring are what the Christian conscience should support. Likewise ERA. And the more women there are in both professional and nonprofessional positions the better.

But there is another facet to the problem of vocation in homemaking which some of the more militant champions of women's liberation overlook. Housekeeping and baby-tending need not be demeaning vocations or the home a prison where talents are manacled or wasted. If the premise of the previous chapter is true, that the stable family unit, whether nuclear or extended, is the crucial cell of a healthy society, the "schoole of souls," as the Puritans called it, where the education or miseducation in values and life-styles takes place, then making a home is a high calling, with rich satisfactions of spirit, where parents as equal partners find their life in losing it for the sake of each other and their children. What they work *at* is housekeeping; what they work *for* is the the vocation of homemaking. Whether one is housewife or househusband, the long pull of often routine and exasperating work so dreary and so daily is redeemed from meaninglessness by the sustaining trust that all the little chores add up to the large purpose of personal fulfillment in making a home where grace and kindness and beauty prevail.

Incidentally, the gracious quality of life at home, as measured in the terms of interpersonal relations, does not depend on the accumulation of gadgets. In fact there may be an *inverse* ratio between the number of mechanical conveniences around and the considerations each member of the circle has for the others. More cars rather than fewer, a quadraphonic stereo system, a food processor, and a cookie gun do not of themselves instill greater sympathy, sensitivity, and concern among the family members. This does not mean that one should throw the electric toaster or the vacuum cleaner in the trashcan. But it does mean that one should be freed from the tyranny of gadgetry, sensibly distinguish real needs from artificial wants, and thus make technology the ally and not the enemy of humanity at home.

Accountability

A final baffling problem remains: how to restore a sense of accountability like that of Luther's carpenter, when the circumstances of fragmentary and mechanical work in our technological society seem to remove all the personal referents of responsibility? The postal clerk sorting mail, the schoolbus driver, the riveter, the janitor, the hematology lab technician, the waitress, the auto mechanic do their work largely unmonitored. The technical ability of a Certified Public Accountant does not in itself certify public accountability. Accountability cannot be legislated from without; only the worst breaches of responsibility in work that may affect health, safety, and welfare come under the jurisdiction of the law. No, accountability must come somehow from within. A conscience responsible in whatever line of work for care, diligence, thoroughness, ingenuity— all the better aspects of the so-called Protestant work ethic—must be cultivated by an inner sense that one's job is crucial to human wellbeing, that it serves to weave and sustain the fabric of community.

Counter to our customary mental habit of "laddering" kinds of work as higher and lower, putting professional work over manual labor, and white-collar over blue-collar jobs, a Christian concept of vocation puts all needful work on a par, as equally worthy in an economy of human interdependence. The care with which my auto mechanic changes the filter on my car is as crucial for the functioning of common life as the care with which I as a teacher should change the filters in the lecture notes for my classes. The cloth sustaining the common good is woven from my trust in your faithful conscience for competence as primary school teacher, yours as housewife, yours as welder on a DC-10, yours as banker, yours as trash collector, yours as personnel manager, yours as sales representative—and yours for mine. St. Paul's analogy of the interdependence of the members of the physical body (1 Cor. 12) is fitting here to the understanding of the equality in interdependence in the humane economy.

A Christian church is the main institution in town which—at least potentially—can cultivate and renew such a sense of accountability and responsibility in work as we have defined it. Despite the customary habit in churches of separating worship from work, worship in its best sense should throw the light of faith upon work, calling those at the altar to remembrance of what their daily work is all about. In worship persons come from many different paths and jobs to hallow the significance of their livelihoods and to lay on the altar, so to speak, the work of their hands, to celebrate anew their interdependence and to be recalled to responsibile service. Worship in this spirit enhances a sense of accountability to God, the deep hidden wellspring of social responsibility.

One might think of many further steps whereby churches might venture out from conventional ways to restore the meaning of vocation to work: industrial chaplaincies, programs for vocational guidance and retraining, inner-city mission projects where the comfortable church in suburbia might assist in tooling unemployed minority groups for worthwhile jobs, or adult discussion groups for the doctors or business executives in the congregation on the ethical problems that arise as they go their workaday rounds. In such ways as these, it may not prove to be so romantic, after all, to relate Christian vocation to everyday work, and to realize again what the Biblical writer meant, describing the farmer and the carpenter: "their prayer is in the practice of their trades." (Ecclus. 38:34)

5

The Fulfillment
of Leisure

> Hell is an endless holiday, the everlasting state of having
> nothing to do and plenty of money to spend on doing it.
> *George Bernard Shaw*

Turn the coin of everyday over to the other side, from "work" to "leisure." Again we discover a welter of ethical problems created by the machineries of the technological revolution with many spin-offs that affect our life-style as much when we are off from work as when we are working.

To look first at the facts: it is plain enough that the major impact of the machine is that it has created mass leisure, long extending the "time-off" portion of the work week. A hundred years ago, the farmer and his wife were at their chores during most of the daylight hours. Currently, in industrial work, the eight-hour shift has become the six-hour or the five-hour shift, and vacation time (with pay) added. And with increased longevity as the consequence of medical science applied in health care, this startling contrast results: whereas a century ago the average working man put in 70 hours a week at the job and lived to be about 40, now the worker puts in about 40 hours per week and can expect to live to be 70. With the time of retirement pushed earlier and earlier by the demands of the economy, both for professional and industrial workers, even despite recent federal legislation proscribing forced retirement at 65, the consequence is the lengthening span of non-work years—ten, fifteen, twenty—of the senior citizens who constitute a growing percent of the American population. In 1870 some 3% of the American population were 65 or older; in 1975, 10.5%. And most of them have little to do but sit and wait it out.

These ratios of time at work and time off from work are not exactly inverse, but are to be qualified by such common practices as "moonlighting," where a person is gainfully employed at two jobs. And in the city-suburb shuttle, does the commuting time by train, bus, or car, consuming 10% to 20% of daylight hours, count as time off or time on? Surely it is not play time at home with the kids. But even taking into account these qualifications, the number of work hours in the week steadily diminishes as machines displace persons. In the estimate of some economists, the twenty-hour work week is a likely "future shock" that should be anticipated now.

Technology has influenced drastically this mass leisure in another fashion: the machine has come to *play* for us, just as it has come to *work* for us. That is, instead of playing ourselves, we watch or listen to others play. Or we come to rely on toys, gadgets, machineries of all sorts, rather than on our own imagination or fancy or muscle to give us fun in our play time. And we pour these toys on our children in the belief that they would be incapable of fun without them.

A Case of Galloping Consumption

This mechanization of recreation is but one sign and symptom of a general trend in the American life-style, namely, a shift from a production-centered to a consumption-centered economy. As leisure time expands, and as the standard of living for most people steadily rises, more and more goods must be sold to serve the comforts, conveniences, and sensate pleasures of more and more people, rather than their bare necessities. A larger and larger portion of the GNP is taken by more toys to play with—whether that be the Aeroscope pictured on the Wheaties box, or the golf cart, or Oil of Olay, or a quadraphonic stereo, or the guided tour to the Caribbees, or just the simple backyard ecstasy of a family barbecue, with a dash of such-and-such a sauce to make it a yummy time for all. Never mind if millions of Americans below the poverty level cannot afford to live it up this way. They nonetheless are in constant sight of the Mechanical Nirvana on the TV screen luring them even if they must go into debt or steal to try to get there.

Its name is consumerism. The power of this force in our economy is evidenced by the gigantic new gray cement shopping center not far from where you live. Little more than two lifetimes ago, the center of town was the village green and its steepled churches, or perhaps the quiet county courthouse square. As the town grew into city and "downtown" meant congestion, the center of gravity moved out to the shopping center. Its very success results in the transfer of the traffic jam, or "artery-sclerosis," from one place to another. Add the complication (and inefficiency!) of the time lost wandering about in the huge parking lot looking for the car. Inside the mall of the shopping center, with its gay decor, its vaguely cheerful and inescapable Musak, even its green plants and splashing fountains, all intended to convey a carnival atmosphere, are offered for sale mountains and mountains of fun goods, few of which anyone really needs but all of which are peddled as though they were every American's birthright. It even has a "Redemption Center," which proves to be not a chapel but a place where you can get even more goodies in exchange for your green stamps that you purchased by paying a little more for the goods you bought at the other stores. As one student of the leisure problem concludes: "In truth, for millions of Americans—*hard-working* Americans—leisure has come to mean little more than an ever more furious orgy of consumption. Whatever energies are left after working are spent in pursuing pleasure with the help of an endless array of goods and services."[1]

In the kingdom of fabricated fun, incidentally, the capital city is Disney World, a sort of Jerusalem, the Holy City for all the devout who come to worship at its castles and shrines. The visitor, having paid the entrance fee, may even receive the sacrament of free grace and blessing from the Christ-figure himself: Mickey Mouse. As a memento, the visitor may have a snapshot taken of the sacred event to bring home. The millions who flock to Disney World and Disneyland, the two most heavily frequented tourist centers in the country, bear witness to the reliance on machine-made fun to fill the empty days and years that mechanized work has dumped on our culture.

The Values at Stake

I have used the word "leisure" thus far to mean "time off" from work, empty time, duration, a quantitative concept. But actually the word "leisure" is a qualitative concept. Leisure may fill time with positive content, rich with meaning and purpose. Aristotle long ago defined leisure as a state of being in which activity is performed for its own sake or as its own end.[2] The significant question is the *value* question: what quality of activity fills our time off work? Are the uses of leisure enriching or impoverishing, degrading or elevating to the human spirit? The vast stretch-out of time off that the machine has brought certainly does not of itself assure that it is put to humanizing use. "Technology has mastered the art of saving time but not the art of spending it."[3] Time may only be something to be "killed." Eric Sevareid once commented that "the most dangerous threat to American society is the *rise of leisure* and the fact that those who have the most leisure are the least equipped to make use of it."[4]

Perhaps the chief value collision that the efficiency of the machine has caused in human play is between active creativity and passivity. A basic element in the Christian view of human nature is carried in the term *homo ludens,* the playing human being. To be fully human means to be alive and alert from within, exercising one's talents, imagination, fancy, body, wit, and skill, whether it be in gardening, sketching, tennis, singing, flying kites, planning a dinner party, jogging, riding a skateboard, knitting, or finding just the right turn of phrase in writing a letter to a friend. But when machines play for us, the slow attrition of passivity sets in, and our spirits die by degrees from the disease of "spectatoritis." It is much easier to watch the efficient tennis professional at Forest Hills on TV than for me as an amateur to get out on the courts with a neighbor friend. TV has not only lowered the literacy rate among the young; it has nearly killed the fine art of conversation in the home. The image of the paunchy, middle-aged man in front of the TV set, beer can in hand, watching the Superbowl game (or "Stuporbowl"), along with 75 million fellow Americans, is a more accurate snapshot of Mr. Middle America at play than the one of him canoeing the rapids, practicing on his cello, or taking the Boy Scout troop on an overnight hike.

The values of freedom and dependence are also at stake here. So ingrained is our reliance on the mechanical devices to assure our comfort and convenience in our workaday life that we carry them all with us even as we talk of "getting away from it all" on vacation. When the family goes to the beach, it takes along all the folding chairs, stereo sets, plastic ice chests, electric grills, rubber rafts, etc.—in effect simply transplanting the cage of things from home to shore. Have you ever examined the mechanical equipment concentrated in a travel trailer? Human dependence on play gadgets, and the nervous, frantic dread that haunts us when deprived of playthings, signal an inner emptiness in the soul, a lack of inner resources of mind and imagination that can travel light and play richly with little or no equipment.

Lifting the Weight of Leisure

If this is at all an accurate picture of the moral problems that technology has built into our use of time off, then our positive concern is now to explore the ways and means of redeeming our life from destruction and of finding the paths out of the wasteland of emptiness and passivity into rich leisure.

As with all the other issues dealt with in this book, it is necessary to repeat the point that technology itself is not the culprit in this story, any more than it is the hero. A technophobia like that of the Luddites, the English industrial workers of the nineteenth century who tried to smash the new factory machineries as threats to their livelihood, is a ridiculous prescription. It is impossible to revert to a pretechnological culture. No, machines can be turned to constructive as readily as to destructive ends. It depends on human choices. "Out of the human heart are the issues of life" (Prov. 4:23, my rendering) still, as it was in Biblical times.

The main moral collision is between creativity and passivity, not between the presence or absence of techniques and toys. In some cases, indeed, it may be necessary to turn off the machine, to escape the cage of things, and move out on one's own spiritual resources, to learn to play oneself, instead of letting the machine do the playing. All sorts of creative play, athletic, aesthetic, and intellectual, are opened by taking initiative. One does not need much equipment to jog, to create beauty and find delight in crochet design or in a garden or in making a footstool at the workbench in the cellar. The alienation experienced in play-life by the machine, which separates and

distances me from what I play at, is overcome by my own invest-
ment. I am reconciled, absorbed in it, doing it "for the fun of it."

The artificial environment of the city shuts me off from nature. In
town I might spend a whole week without once setting foot on soil,
seeing a single star in the night sky, or hearing the call of a bird. To
escape this artificial prison into the green of woods or the white of
ocean spray and resume contact with the natural rhythms of the tides
and the seasons is to find one's soul restored. Wilderness and the
grace of green quicken again the sense of wonder, awe, pristine delight and reverence, sensibilities at the heart of *homo ludens* and the
religious imagination. If work-life in the city spells wreck-creation,
time close to the earth and the primal elements spells re-creation.

The technological mentality is hardheaded, factual, precise, suspi-
cious of myth and fantasy. Yet one essential habit of *homo ludens* is
the gift for whim, fantasy, make-believe, odd fancy, and wild imagin-
ings. If all there is to human existence, in work or play, is to cope
with its bare facts, to reduce all fable to empirical fact, it would be a
dreary and sodden business indeed. The fantastic is as necessary to
the life abundant as is the factual. The capacity to play by expressing
and enjoying fantasy and fancy is a much needed therapy to enrich
the empty leisure of middle and late years. Children at play have a
spontaneous capacity for make-believe, charades, and fantasy. When
Christ affirmed that those who would enter the kingdom must turn
and become as little children, perhaps this is one childlike quality he
implied.

There is also a social dimension to the phenomenon of leisure.
Social creatures that we are, usually we play together with others and
come to rely on company to fill the void of empty hours. To be deprived of *some* kind of interpersonal contact, we feel, is to be cast
into the dread abyss of loneliness.

Surely the loneliness of the elderly, the friendless and bereaved
widow, facing the desolation of empty hours in an empty house or in
a nursing home, is a bitter experience. These persons need the conso-
lations of caring friends.

Yet there is a subtle moral difference between loneliness and solitude. The former is a negative experience, a void, an absence. The
latter *may* be a positive experience. Liberated from dependence on

present company, one can cultivate the inner resources of mind and aesthetic enrichment, keeping company with a distant host of writers or painters or musicians in the past, and know their companionship in the serenity, the "bliss" of solitude. Such self-sufficiency St. Paul describes when he speaks of learning "how to abound; in any and all circumstances . . . [when] facing plenty and hunger, abundance and want." (Phil. 4:12) "Solitary" need not mean "confinement" for one whom the fortunes of life have forced to live alone.

Especially is this true for the elderly, as students of geriatrics have long observed. While the margins of physical activity gradually close in, the margins of the spirit can open out with passing years. Those persons who have the intellectual and aesthetic resources to compensate for physical frailties remain "young in spirit."

The ways of restoration here proposed are ways which do not require technology to fulfill our leisure time. But certainly there are many resources which *do* use human machines to dignify and enrich off-hours. Most prominently, the mass media, especially TV and radio, are potential resources for bringing the glorious cultural heritage of music and literatures, scientific discovery and lore, marvelous adventures of mind and spirit, into every home, especially those of the elderly and housebound. The machine itself is not responsible for the quality of the fare it conveys; that is a matter of the producer's choices. The printing press can turn out poetry as efficiently as pornography, and the stereo Bach or schlock. The kings of television can produce "Kojak" or "Masterpiece Theatre." In protest against the dehumanizing effect of the junk shows of commercial TV, schooling its young viewers in the ways of violence, sex, and sensate materialism, the recent growth of public broadcasting has much improved matters. The enrichment of great theater, great music, great art, great history is now available at the turn of the knob. TV educational programs, too, are the redemption of leisure. They build on the correct premise that one is never too young or never too old to grow in mind.

As it can be the instrument of the recovery of vocation in work, as was indicated in chapter 4, even more so the church can be an instrument for the fulfillment of leisure. An essential part of its ministry to young people is to lead them out from a dependence on things that play for them to discover the delight of playing themselves. Interchurch softball or basketball leagues, the presentation for the congregation or at the retirement home of a dramatic version of a Biblical episode, or an interpretive dance group are but a few examples of creative leisure for teenagers. The church's ministry to the senior citizens who constitute a growing portion of its membership might involve a program of creative play suited to the limits of their years. A choral group, a play-reading club, a quilting circle, a writing project on the history of the local congregation, and guided tours of the art museum, are examples of the ways that the years of retirement can be turned from death to life and God's name again be praised.

6

The Ethics
of Communication

> Insofar as people . . . make watching it [TV] a habit and take its drama at all seriously, it insinuates chiefly hollow or false values, cheapens the quality of life, muddies rather than clarifies their own experience. . . . Above all, it impoverishes life. It dulls the capacity of people for wonder and awe.
>
> *Herbert J. Muller*

Two scenes in sharp contrast:

Scene A: A remote, barren, primitive hamlet on the borders of Philistine country in eighth-century B.C. Palestine. A few ragged villagers eke out a bleak existence from the poor soil. They cannot read or write. They live in tents or barely habitable huts of mud and mortar. Their lives, plagued by famine and disease, are fleeting and brief. One of their number, a prophet named Micah, speaks some words to a few who remember them and pass them on in the oral tradition: "What doth the LORD require of thee, but to do justly, and to love mercy, and to walk humbly with thy God?" (Micah 6:8, KJV)

Scene B: 1977. Standing in a solar-heated platform before the Capitol in Washington, well-clothed, well-fed, protected by a bulletproof glass partition, President Carter takes the oath of office and then, addressing the whir of the TV cameras, repeats these same words: "He hath showed thee what is good: and what doth the Lord require of thee, but to do justly, to love mercy, and to walk humbly with thy God?" Thousands of miles away you see and hear this image in color, sitting comfortably in your playroom, you and millions of other Americans.

The same words. But the medium of communication has been so drastically changed, as have so many other cultural and technological forces between Scene A and Scene B, that the meaning and the import of the words themselves are altered, even though Jimmy Carter calls the words a "timeless admonition." What comes between Scene A and Scene B is the technological revolution, profoundly influencing still another human activity, namely communication, and with it the moral terms of community. *What* persons communicate to each other is colored and reshaped by *how* they communicate, by the medium used, to the extent that, as Marshall McLuhan says, with a good measure of truth, "the medium *is* the message." My interest in this phase of the technological revolution is with its import for Christian morality, for the problems of responsibility and accountability in truth-telling and with the qualities of trust or distrust which sustain or tear the fabric of interpersonal relations.

The Three Eras of Communication

The three main epochs in the history of communication are well known: (1) oral, (2) print, and (3) electronic. Oral communication, of course, is person-to-person, face-to-face. Where messages and meanings are transmitted in this manner, the situation is one of intimacy, directness, and candor. The context makes for dialogue back and forth. Though credibility is not guaranteed, the context and mode of exchange are more likely to assure sincerity, accountability, and responsibility, where persons say what they mean and mean what they say.

In the Jewish community of the faithful (Scene A), there was also a vertical dimension in communication. It was a Divine Monitor, "who looketh on the heart," to whom one was accountable both for the words of the mouth and the meditations of the heart, or, as Psalm 139 puts it, "Even before a word is on my tongue . . . O LORD, thou knowest it altogether." To be sure, the Bible speaks often of deceit and hypocrisy, practices as endemic to human behavior then as now, but normatively, the awareness of the divine Lie Detector sensitized the conscience to responsibility in speaking the truth, "to be as good as one's word." In our secular society, the last vestige and ghost of this vertical accountability remains in the court procedure of taking an oath on the Bible, "to speak the truth, the whole truth, and nothing but the truth." Presumably this assures credibility.

The oral mode of communication was first the only and then the main type from the very beginning up through the fifteenth century. With Gutenberg, the invention of movable type, and the printing press, a major revolution took place. In this second epoch of communication by the *printed* word, the reach of ideas was extended far out beyond what even shouted words could register. Literacy and education rose for the masses, and the power of ideas to influence action through print increased exponentially. The horizons of awareness opened out, both in time and space, way beyond the confines of Micah's reach or that of his hearers.

When communication is by printed word, both the sender and receiver move in a linear progression of thought. The transaction is rational. The reader may weigh, ponder, savor, measure, agree or disagree with what is read. In one sense, print reduces the dialogic character of oral communication, yes, but it does not eliminate the power of sender and receiver to discriminate and respond. Print draws the mind of the reader to the internal logic and worth of the words or moves his or her emotions with their aesthetic beauty. And in our own day, with the "publication explosion," as more and more books, magazines, newspapers are at hand, the reader's freedom to choose what messages he or she will absorb is vastly extended, to the point indeed where the glut of words is overwhelming.

The third revolution in communication has taken place only in the last sixty years or so. Its spiritual and moral consequences no one can yet measure, but strong signals are coming through that technology in this form is changing radically the human heart and consciousness. Of the various forms of the electronic media (sound: telephone and radio; vision *and* sound: movies and television), television has come in thirty years' time almost to monopolize the communications market.

The bare statistics are startling. 98% of American homes have one or more TV sets, turned on more than six hours every day—2300 hours a year. Children under 5 watch an average of 23.5 hours of TV a week. Adults average about 44 hours. One study of the matter claims that the average American is exposed to 1600 ads each day and 10,000 TV commercials a year.[1] There is something on from 6 in the morning through the late, late movie after midnight. Half of the characters on prime-time TV are involved in violence, 10% in killings. There are about 16 violent scenes an hour in children's programs. The circulation of *TV Guide* is the second largest of any magazine in the country. One wonders how long it will be, at this rate, before the public libraries of America will become museums.

The very structure of the electronic media changes the character of what is communicated from the linear, rational progression of the printed words to the visual, instantaneous impact of vision and sound in TV. It is more vivid than the abstract word, but it narrows if not precludes the chance for reflection, analysis, "reviewability." The wide freedom for the reader to choose what he or she will attend to is now cut back to the options among at most 4 or 5 channels. Though cable television and CB radio are beginning to open out the choices for sender and receiver, such a high monopolization of power in so few centers, controlling the flow of signals to millions of Americans, is a fact of grave ethical weight. Moreover, in contrast to the epoch of oral communication, which is dialogic, TV is monologic: one-way. There is no feedback, response, exchange. Finally, the TV camera eye focuses on the external, the appearance, the front, so that the attention of the viewer is distracted by the outward image, the grin, the hairdo, or the costume, from the internal meaning of what is conveyed. What is carried and remembered from the shot of the president signing a tax bill on the White House lawn may be the number of pens used in signing it rather than the likely impact of the bill on the future American economy.

Contending Values in the Mass Media

Life in almost every American home goes on under the sign of the cross. But the cross is a TV aerial, not the cross of Christ. This is empirical fact. But how much it is also a moral evaluation is a moot question. It would be fatuous to claim that the mass media, the press, radio, and TV in particular, have no influence in shaping moral values —that they are merely ethically neutral channels for conveying news and providing entertainment. On the contrary, TV has become the main moral educator in the home, "the flickering blue parent," as it has been called. Its barrage of messages instills a certain syndrome of qualities which are taken to constitute the good life. At some points these are consonant with Christian morality; at many more points they stand in opposition.

For one thing, the daily flood of commercials instructs the young and the old in the gospel of scientism. If the *Rule of St. Benedict,* a Christian classic of medieval monasticism, was a manual for conscience guiding the believer in the ascetic paths of poverty, chastity, obedience, reverence, humility, and charity, the Rule of Madison Avenue is a manual for the conscience of the American consumer, enticing us toward comfort, convenience, glamor, speed, and sensate pleasure as the true paths of righteousness. These are the supreme values. To realize these is to find the life abundant. "After all," as the Geritol ad used to say, "if you've got your health, you've got just about everything." (This was *not* one of the seven last words of Christ on the cross.)

For another thing, the TV camera and the newspaper are drawn to the sensational, to the violent, to the bizarre. A news account of the average day's activity of a New Jersey housewife, shopping, reading, taxiing her children, cooking, etc., would not even get as far as the copy editor's desk, but a blackout in New York City, with stores looted or destroyed—that is front-page news. The Parisian reader comes to think that this is New York's regular life-style, just as Americans might come to think that terrorism is commonplace in Italy. Why are the daytime shows on TV jammed with scenes of violence? Partly because the TV camera cannot depict Plato contemplating a Pure Idea, but it *can* catch movement, the action in "Kojak" of a shoot-out or a fistfight. On the average, an American youth will have witnessed 18,000 TV murders by the time he or she has completed high school. The moral result is inevitably the belief that violence is a normal way to get what you're after in life. In a Florida court a fifteen-year-old murderer was defended with the claim that he was an innocent victim of "involuntary TV addiction" to violence.

Another sort of value collision accentuated by the electronic media, alluded to in the previous chapter, is between the values of active creativity and passivity. TV is one-directional. The receiver has no chance for reply or rebuttal. He or she is doped into dull passivity, "spectatoritis," as I have called it. The family members let the machine play for them and gradually lose the art of play itself. This is especially dangerous for children. As one *Newsweek* article put it,

> The time kids spend sitting catatonic before the set has been exacted from such salutary pursuits as reading, outdoor play, even simple, contemplative solitude. TV prematurely jades, rendering passé the normal experiences of growing up.[2*]

The whole matter of objectivity versus subjectivity, truth versus deceit, impartiality versus bias in the mass media is much too complex to more than sketch here, but surely the dialectical tension of values is evident. On the one hand, the fast electronic media are able to present reality in news broadcasts with the directness of immediate evidence, "to see it like it is," to send the portrait of reality "warts and all." "Pictures don't lie." On the other hand, even a novice in journalism well knows that biases and slants permeate newswriting and newscasting. Even the camera angle in the choice of the photographer can present the subject in a favorable or unfavorable light. Malcolm Muggeridge reports that during the filming of a Nixon commercial in 1972, the floor manager was instructed to keep the witch hazel handy, for "We can't do the sincerity bit if he's sweating."[3] The choice of what items of news to report on CBS Nightly News and what to drop from among the deluge pouring into the studio involves the slant of the newscaster or anchorman about what is significant. The tube is not a neutral lens through which everyone sees just "how it is." The main criterion of what is significant is the newscaster's system of values.

A Christian Estimate

Already it is plain that this assessment of the values at stake is itself not descriptively neutral, but is already slanted by a Christian value bias. Let us now examine directly the impact of the electronic media on the consciousness of America from a Christian viewpoint.

There are both benefits and costs to the human spirit in television and radio. They are both humanizing and brutalizing. On the positive side, TV can be credited with a liberation of persons from narrow provincialism and a myopic view of the world. The telecast brings me nightly news of what is happening in Ireland, in Rhodesia, in Berlin, in Brazil, emancipating me from a prison of ignorance about what life is like outside the bounds of my little village. It makes the world a global village, at least in the sense that I am made aware of the fortunes, good or bad, of all members of the human family. Though this generation of youngsters, hooked on what's up-to-the-minute news, may suffer from myopia in *time* and lack the perspective of history, they are far less insular in *space* and know far more about their present world than their elders did when they were young.

TV and radio have also made available to millions as never before the vast riches of a cultural heritage in music, dance, drama, poetry, literature, history. For those housebound, the elderly, the hospital patient, Vivaldi, or Ibsen, or Chekhov, Mozart, or Beethoven is there to fill empty hours with beauty and meaning. Educational programs for children can make learning for them an exciting experience. Educational programs for adults, too, in science and history, broaden the horizons of the mind and bring the cold abstractions of the textbook alive. The TV series on *Roots*, for example, did more to bring home to the conscience of the white American the cruelties of the slave system and the reasons for black rage than the textbook course in race relations in American history could possibly do. And the series on *The Holocaust* brought that tragedy alive. Surely these are all factors on the *plus* side of the moral ledger.

On the *minus* side, however, there are many points where the mass media in general and TV in particular violate Christian ethical norms and are dehumanizing in their effect. Despite the apparent vividness and directness of TV communication, there is another sense in which the machine blocks communication and alienates the sender from the receiver. Unlike oral communication, there is no dialogue, no feedback. Unlike communication by the printed word, TV is instantaneous and fleeting, allowing for no review or assessment. Consequently its appeal is more to the emotions than to the mind. The very nature of the medium itself lends itself to propaganda, the mass engineering of consent, rather than deliberated response. As one critic put it,

> the fact is that television's dependence on pictures . . . makes it not only a *powerful* means of communication, but a *crude* one which tends to strike at the emotions rather than at the intellect. For TV journalism this means a . . . concentration on action (usually violent and bloody) rather than on thought, on happenings rather than issues, on shock rather than explanation, on personalities rather than ideas.[4]

The worst moral violation in commercial TV appears in the gross or subtle deceits of advertising, often the more vicious because the more sly. The new Buick Galaxy sitting out on the shoreline cliff, with a gorgeous blonde in long white evening gown leaning seductively on its fenders, suggests subliminally that the blonde comes with the car. (The male middle-aged customer who might buy it is subconsciously disappointed to find that she doesn't.) Or the auto ads always show the car on the open road, *never* in traffic. Aftershave lotion is peddled on the basis of its sex appeal, and face lotions because of their rejuvenating powers. Granted, as an old axiom of advertising has it, "It's the sizzle, not the cow, that sells the steak." Yet these monstrous deceptions in advertising assail millions daily and create a credibility gap for the medium itself.

Another sly bit of advertising witchcraft is the scene set in an old-fashioned small town General Store, where Fred, suffering from back pain or headache, encounters friend Charlie, the solicitous clerk. Instant relief is assured in fifteen seconds by a bond of personal trust between clerk and customer that validates the nostrum. In real life, of course, the purchase of such magic potions goes on in the huge supermarket, where nobody knows anybody. This hardly squares with any Christian criterion of truth-telling. Some time ago, the Federal Communications Commission denied a license to a TV station that promoted programs of astrology, sorcery, and witchcraft. No one has raised any protest against the sorcery and witchcraft that prevail in the commercials on the main licensed channels day and night.

Moreover, the monologic character of the medium induces passivity in the mind of the viewer or at least makes difficult a creative positive response. The machine does our thinking for us. It does not call forth imagination, wit, or mental skill. It does not throw the question to us but gives us the fabricated answer. For that reason TV is credited by educators as one of the chief factors in lowering dangerously the literacy rate among young Americans, as measured by declining SAT scores. And though there is no way to measure the matter statistically, one cannot help but feel that it has also lowered the rate of skill in dialogic conversation in the home, in honing the mind to think carefully and critically by engaging in discourse. Certainly it is not conducive to family devotions and ritual. Father and mother once thought it would be nice to say grace at the dinner table, but since it proved rather awkward to interrupt Walter Cronkite and the evening news, the family grace was soon omitted.

Another damaging effect of TV is the frequency of scenes of violence, not only on the soap operas, but on the news as well. Scenes of rioting in Ulster or Rhodesia are newsworthy; scenes of peace and domestic tranquillity are not. One might argue that the newscasts from Vietnam brought home to the American citizen, as no newspaper account could do, the horror of the Vietnam War and helped turn the tide of American sentiment against our policy there. But no one could argue that the frequency with which violence prevails on daytime shows constitutes a healthy form of moral education for children.

All in all, it would seem, the impact of commercial TV on the value-structure of Mr. and Mrs. Middle America and their children represents more an allegiance to the faith of scientism and the blessings of consumerism and the kicks of brutality than to the Christian faith. The good life celebrated on commercial TV consists in sensate enjoyment of creature comforts and maximum efficiency, convenience, and speed. The tragic dimensions of life—death, pain, sorrow, anguish of spirit, hatred—are bracketed out or reduced to minor malfunctioning. "Why, everybody has trouble falling asleep now and then. That's why I take Sominex." This blithe and reassuring ad never mentions the horror of sleepless nights for those who are bereaved, who are taut with worry about a prodigal son, whose morale is shattered by a marriage breaking apart. In these cases, Sominex will hardly suffice. The Christian values of tenderness, patience, sacrificial love, trust, humility, reverence, responsibility to God—in short, the cardinal values of our religious heritage are rarely given their due.

It is significant to note the wide gap between the norms set for television producers in the national Television Code,[5] many of which reflect traditional Christian values, and the actual day-by-day level of material that appears.

> Television and all who participate in it are jointly accountable to the American public for respect for the special needs of children, for community responsibility, for the advancement of education and culture, . . . for decency and decorum in production, and for propriety in advertising. . . .
>
> Such subjects as violence and sex shall be presented without undue emphasis. . . .
>
> Material which is excessively violent or would create morbid suspense, or other undesirable reactions in children, should be avoided.

How does the record square with *that* standard?

> Program materials should enlarge the horizons of the viewer, provide him with wholesome entertainment, . . . and remind him of the responsibilities which the citizen has towards his society.

When have you seen a program reminding you of your responsibility toward your society?

> The presentation of cruelty, greed, and selfishness as worthy motivations is to be avoided.

On the morning quiz show, the young housewife is promised $5000 if she can name the capital of Sweden. She guesses correctly and bursts into joyous rapture at earning the jackpot. How does such a scene square with this last norm?

Redeeming the Mass Media

As with the other modes of the technological revolution I have discussed, a Christian normative response is not a redemption *from* technology but a redemption *of* technology, turning its wheels from dehumanizing to humanizing ends. A crusade of militant church folk who would go from house to house throwing all TV sets and radios into the street would be futile and silly. No, we must recall again that there are persons behind the machine deciding about the quality of the fare that goes forth on the airwaves. If the broadcasters claim "we give the people what they want," it is incumbent for an aroused group of citizens, church people and others, to protest the garbage spewed forth—especially the excessive violence as the National PTA has done—and to voice their better wants to the producers. There is nothing in the medium itself which prevents the communication of humane values. Tenderness, compassion, sympathy, patience, trust— these Christian virtues can be made as photogenic and compelling as violence and brutality. TV can teach children cooperation as readily as it can teach them cruelty.

One of the most promising recent developments in the mass media is the rise in popularity and support for public radio and TV. Here, uncluttered by offensive ads, programming of high quality brings a richness of fare uplifting to the human spirit, redeeming life from the drab and the dross. More and more frequently, too, public TV and radio provide programs that analyze in depth current issues of foreign policy, or the state of economy, or the crisis in the American family structure. In back-and-forth exchange of opposing points of view, in forum or debate, something of the dialogic character of communication is restored, and the viewer is enticed to reflect and measure critically public issues, to examine why he or she agrees or disagrees. Also, structured TV classes and courses in foreign languages, arts and crafts, even sciences, can overcome the passivity of spectatoritis and incite active response.

Finally, if, as the Television Code puts it, TV should remind the viewer "of the responsibilities which the citizen has towards his society," then public TV can arouse the Christian conscience toward an awareness of the rights and needs of the human family around the globe and the rights of the good earth itself. The sight of near-naked children with bloated stomachs, starving to death in a sub-Sahara desert village, or the vision of Alaska wilderness threatened by "developers," or of black teenagers looting a Brooklyn store, can bring home to the moral imagination the vast extent of human and natural need. It may recover a sense of stewardship for the good earth and the far neighbor, and restore a sense of accountability to the One who requires that we should "do justly, love mercy, and walk humbly with thy God."

7
The Energy Crisis

> The world has achieved brilliance without wisdom, power without conscience. Ours is a world of nuclear giants and ethical infants.
>
> *General Omar Bradley*

We can assume that those gathered in this room have so far today arisen from sleep in air-conditioned or well-heated homes or dormitories, showered, shaved or possibly used an electric hair-blower, consumed a breakfast cooked on three different electric appliances, and, if a bit late in getting to the adult class at church, put the dishes in the electric dishwasher, or, if dashing from a campus cafeteria to a nine o'clock class, thrown away the disposable cups, spoons, plates in the bins as they left. To get here probably required driving the car, usually one person per car, perhaps quite a distance. Each of these actions taken together used up how many kilowatts of electricity and how many gallons of petroleum and water? And the day has hardly begun. How many more units of energy will be consumed before the day is over?

But no one arrives at class haggard or twitching with a guilty conscience. These actions are hardly vicious. On the contrary, are they not done with the benign moral purpose of learning something about Christian ethics? What could be more moral than that?

But if we refocus the camera lens from this close-up snapshot out to infinity, to see how things look from a transcendent perspective, the morality of the matter may appear somewhat different. While this class discussion is going on, an eight-year-old child in a village of the sub-Sahara desert in Africa is walking three miles through baking heat from the nearest well to her family's hut, carrying the single bucket of water which must do for the drinking, cooking, and washing needs of her family for the night. And at dawn in the city of

Calcutta in India, an ox-drawn cart moves slowly through the back alleys of the city's hovels. Onto the cart are thrown the corpses of the infants and the aged who have died during the night. The world around, 10,000 people die every day from starvation and the diseases coming from malnutrition.

Viewed in this perspective, the life-style of these students sitting here comfortably in class may not prove quite so benign and innocent. When one compares the degrees of energy consumption among different members of the human family, the contrasts are startling. Americans constitute 6% of the world's population: they use 40% to 50% of the world's natural resources. The cars and trucks on the New Jersey Turnpike at peak load-time consume as much energy in one *minute* as the whole nation of Zaire uses in one *day*. The average American adult exhausts 50 times the amount of energy used by a child in Rhodesia.

Already in these percentages there loom some moral issues concerning the distribution of energy the world around. But just to limit ourselves to the dynamics of the American economy itself, it is plain that the energy crisis, as a by-product of the technological revolution, is one of the most urgent issues facing persons of conscience, Christian or not, who dare to look out from the cozy confines of their nest of things to see how precariously it is perched on the branch of existence, indeed, how endangered is the species *homo sapiens* itself. If viewed in the large, the issue is not one of more versus less comfort and convenience, or even of striking a balance between supply and demand, but of human survival.

As we have traced the story in previous chapters, in the industrial revolution the machine produced the factory, and the factory produced the modern industrial city, with its close concentration of populations. The economy of the city requires in turn high amounts of energy to turn the wheels of transportation of workers back and forth from work to home, as the distance stretches from where people work to where they live. The dynamics of the economy demand, it would seem, an ever-mounting production of goods and services, the cornucopia of blessings supplied by the abundant society. Up into the middle of this century it was generally and blandly assumed that the world's energy supply, domestic and foreign, was inexhaustible. Only a few prophetic warning voices were raised. The American public went merrily on its upward energy-consuming ride, at the annual rate of 4% to 6%, for business and pleasure, to light, heat, and cool homes and factories, to ride in more and bigger cars and airplanes toward the destination of the Kingdom of Happiness. Then in 1973–74 came the OPEC embargo of oil and the fourfold price increase. For a few citizens, this was an alert to the perils of America's dependence on Arab oil imports. For the majority, it was an annoying interruption in the morning's usual routine to have to queue up at the gas pumps. After the embargo and shortage passed, Americans went back to big cars and high gas consumption, with a few grumbles about higher prices but little concern for the poor who suffer the most from inflation. Then the fuel supply for home heating fell dangerously short in the winter of 1977–78, but somehow we managed to cope. Now, however, other dimensions of the energy crisis are being brought home to public consciousness. With Iran's political upheaval in 1979, the crisis became more acute, as the summer gas supply ran very short.

President Carter's energy program was a carefully orchestrated attempt to coordinate supply, demand, and costs with minimal hurt to producers, consumers, and environment. The debate which his program sparked in and out of Congress, and the compromised legislation that finally emerged, are sobering illustrations of many of the themes of this book: the implicit trust in technology as savior, the assumption, largely unchallenged, that maximum speed, power, comfort, and convenience are the ultimate goals of human existence, the refusal to acknowledge that the earth's resources are finite and that our technological culture has reached if not exceeded these limits. The debate also confirms vividly the Christian understanding of human nature. The devious ways that self-interested bias twists even the reading of the facts to favor private wants over public needs: utility company executives to be assured of high profit, consumer groups to be assured of maximum convenience at minimum cost, and all parties favoring high consumption now with little concern for the needs of posterity or the rights of the earth. The name of the game, to use a classic Christian term, is "original sin."

The Hard Facts

Whatever one's biases, there are certain empirical facts that are unavoidable.[1] The first is that the American economy is increasingly energy-intensive. In 1970 we used twice the amount of energy used in 1950. The likelihood is that energy use will grow annually by 4%, to double again by the year 2000. The second fact is the enormous waste of energy in American consumption patterns. The third fact is that the United States has in the last few years grown increasingly reliant on oil, at the close of 1976 about 42% imported. The OPEC cartel jumped the price per barrel fourfold, putting the importing nations, as one commentator quipped, "quite literally over the barrel." A fourth fact is that the supply of natural gas and oil which together give us 77% of our energy is running low and will have run out, at our present rate of use, by the year 2000 or soon after. Offshore drilling, extended distances of transport, and such expensive ventures as the Alaska pipeline increase the risk and rate of oil-spills and environmental damage, to a degree, though not quantifiable, horrendous to imagine. Each new technological solution, it seems, brings in its wake new problems just as serious as the ones "solved." The authors of the Club of Rome report call this "negative feedback."[2]

In the face of these facts, the utility companies are turning toward other sources as the only possible way to solve the dilemma of mounting energy demands and diminishing resources of natural gas and oil. One source, of course, is the coal that in 1900 gave us 73% of our power, used then to turn many fewer wheels. The other source is nuclear energy. Its advocates claim that the conjurer's magic of high technology has provided the panacea for all energy problems in the trick of nuclear fission. In comparison to oil, natural gas, and coal as energy sources, nuclear energy, it is claimed, is clearly preferable: it is cheap, readily accessible from an adequate supply of uranium ore, and provides, say its advocates, a maximum yield of power with a minimum input of ore and little risk to environment or the lives and health of persons. The Messiah has come. Nuclear energy will save us from darkness and deep freeze.

But now dispute arises concerning even the *facts* of nuclear energy and its effects. In the thick of the debate—about various techniques of nuclear fission and cooling systems, the degree of safety in reprocessing or storing plutonium, which is the highly toxic by-product of uranium fission, the cost-benefit trade-off of non-breeder reactors versus breeder reactors, pollution control and protection against melt-down—the non-technician soon becomes lost in the jungle of technical information. Nobel Prize physicists muster "objective" data to support opposing policies. Some warn that to go down the road of the addition of nuclear plants, as now planned and under construction, is to go to death and destruction. Other physicists insist that "The hazards [in breeder reactors using plutonium] are real enough, but there is little to suggest that they are beyond control, or that they are disproportionately large either in relation to non-nuclear hazards or to values to be derived from nuclear energy. The fact is that plutonium has been processed, stored, and used in large quantities since 1945 without serious accident."[3] The *Reactor Safety Study* of the Nuclear Regulatory Commission (known as the Rasmussen Report) claimed that it has been proven safe.[4] However, in 1979 the Nuclear Regulatory Commission revised its earlier approval of the Rasmussen Report: the degree of safety was actually much lower and the hazards much greater. Then came the Three Mile Island accident.

Well, whom should I believe, the Union of Concerned Scientists who say, "The commerical nuclear power plant program planned for the next 25 years in this country represents a serious threat to your health and safety and to the health and safety of the American people,"[5] or the proponents of more nuclear power plants? Which bumper-sticker should I heed: "No Nukes Is Good Nukes" or "Let the Bastards Freeze to Death in the Dark"?

The Values at Stake

Close underneath the surface of the physical facts lurk values in collision and human and extra-human factors that cannot be quantified in any cost-benefit equation. The most obvious is the clash between the good of high productivity of goods and services, providing employment and income for more and more people, versus the resources of earth needed to power the machines that turn out these goods and services. The abundant economy wars with the abundance of the earth.

Another value clash will intensify when oil and natural gas run low and coal and nuclear energy become likely options. Both of these latter threaten the values of life and health: coal, since its burning pollutes the air through sulfur, and since with heavy use it traps the carbon dioxide in the atmosphere, as though in a greenhouse, raising the mean temperature of the earth even to the level that slowly melts the polar icecaps. And mining endangers the health of miners with black-lung disease. Nuclear energy greatly increases the risks of accidents in storing the waste of the nuclear reactor plants, especially plutonium. It takes plutonium half a million years to lose its killing power. Where can all this lethal waste be stored safely for so long?

In the safety-risk trade-off, incidentally, the choices for a technological society are not between a risky and a riskless life, but among kinds and degrees of risks that are high no matter what. It has been estimated that the chances of a person being killed in an auto accident are about 4000 to 1; in a nuclear accident, 5 billion to 1. So, take your chances.

Another dimension of the values at stake, especially in the nuclear energy debate, is the social dimension: who gains and who suffers? The developing nations of the world, no longer able to afford Arab oil and in desperate need of nuclear energy technology to lift their bleak economy, turn to the seven nuclear exporting nations, one of which is the U.S.A., for nuclear technique and for ore. Yet, as nuclear capabilities are extended out and out, with no strong international system of surveillance even in prospect, the dangers of sabotage and terrorism and nuclear blackmail are increased. What assurance is there that a nation will not turn its nuclear technology from peaceful uses to make a nuclear bomb? If an MIT sophomore could show how it might be done (as one actually did), could not a terrorist group in Northern Ireland or Lebanon? As one World Council of Churches report put it, "The necessity to maintain international safeguards while allowing the unrestrained expansion of nuclear energy for civil purposes is a major paradox at the centre of the nuclear power debate."[6]

Still another sharp value collision in the debate is between quantity of consumption and quality of consumption. The demand for the quick and ready energy provided by nuclear power is based on the assumption that America must produce and consume more and more material goods and services. The GNP line *must* rise, it is claimed, else our economy would fall into a shambles. If this is true, then we need an ethic of high consumerism, with a rapid turnover of goods, built-in obsolescence that assures the turnover of new gadgets to replace the worn-out ones, and the persuasion by advertisers that what our grandparents would regard as luxuries are really necessities. The pretty young housewife testifies to all her viewers on TV, whether rich or poor, that she doesn't know how in the world she managed before she got her microwave oven. The amount of baggage which the parents of the university freshman bring in September in the back of the station wagon (or maybe even in a U-Haul trailer), and that he regards as bare necessities in his survival kit, is considerably more than what Thomas Carlyle carried on his back in walking the eighty miles from his home in Scotland to enroll as a freshman at the University of Edinburgh. Many American students—perhaps most— are convinced that it is impossible to get a good undergraduate education without having a car on campus.

Such high energy consumption, with all its attendant waste, collides with another value strong in our Puritan-Yankee heritage: the spiritual value of simplicity in life-style, the frugality sensitive to the difference between real needs and artificial wants. There may not be an inevitable positive correlation between "plain living and high thinking," but there are certain qualitative values of human sensitivity and concern and sanity of perspective in the ascetic tradition that knows how to do without physical things to be rich in spirit.

This word, incidentally, is addressed not to those who are below the poverty level, as though to say, "It's good for your character to do without." Rather, it is addressed to the vast majority of Americans above the poverty level who just assume without much thought that "more is better."

There are serious political and economic dimensions to this dilemma. Both the federal government and the giant utilities have invested so many billions in nuclear plants that they are loath to reverse themselves and reinvest in solar power. Photoelectric technology—which does not need vast land space—is a live option, but is resisted by power companies. The president's 1979 budget offers signs of hope, however, in the millions it proposes for solar energy research and development. The sun may prove to be "pie in the sky" after all.

There are many other value collisions snarled in the energy crisis: the value of political and economic interdependence of all nations of the world versus the value of American self-sufficiency, not dependent on the fortune of Arab powers for its basic energy resources. Or the time dimension: the demand for quick energy *now* and in the immediate decades ahead—necessary before technology can develop less environmentally destructive sources of energy, like solar, wind, and geothermal—may be satisfied, but only at the very high price of the suffering of posterity. Certainly the energy needs of future generations must be weighed against the needs of the present generation, and in an economy inevitably scarce one option must be preferred at the sacrifice of the other. Within the closing limits of supply, it becomes a cruel either-or dilemma.

Christian Wisdom for Energy Dilemmas

At first glance, the norms of Christian ethics seem entirely remote from this tangle of technical problems. What in the world does the Bible have to say about thorium, plutonium, uranium 235, or to the problem of nuclear proliferation, to the merits of various techniques of nuclear fission, to breeder reactors versus non-breeder reactors? The Bible does say early on "Let there be light," yes, but in answering the technical problems as to how light may be provided for our technological society it is silent. Therefore, we go not to the church or pastor for the answers, but to the lab or the engineering school, to the nuclear physicists. They will point us to the well-lighted path of salvation.

Yet, as with all the other problems we have discussed, when confronted with the value questions, when asked what *ought* we do, the technicians are baffled, for nothing in the facts or the graphs themselves prescribes the answer to the question about moral ends.

Moreover, much of the debate about nuclear energy is faulty in that it leaves out of account the human factor. It is so preoccupied with technical matters and machines that it fails to see live persons standing there, making decisions about the uses of their machines. Persons are used by machines, not vice versa. So, for example, if the line of energy consumption rises exponentially, then policy decisions about energy must keep up with that line, and persons must accommodate their wants and needs to what that line prescribes. Such a technological determinism would deny the premise that human beings have a measure of choice about how much energy they will consume and that another life-style of conservation, consciously willed from within, might turn the line in the direction of lowered energy use.

When one looks behind the machine to the persons who decide about its uses, there is indeed wisdom from the Christian faith that can inform decisions and choices about energy. Recall the basic Biblical moral norm of the stewardship of earth: the basic resources of nature are to be employed to serve the needs of humanity as the expression of responsible love. Nature is to be used to serve the neighbor out of reverent love of God. Several implications of this moral norm bear on the energy problem:

1. All the rich resources of earth—soil, forest, ore, fossil fuels, ocean, wind, sun—are gifts of God's continual beneficence, to be used reverently and responsibly. Nature is not to be worshiped itself as God. Neither is it to be plundered or exploited.

2. Human technologies in developing modes of energy are not themselves to be adored as God, nor abhorred as demonic, but to be pursued within a moral frame of reference that employs techniques yielding the maximum energy for the widest range of human needs with the minimal damage to the environment. Those forms of energy production where risks of catastrophe clearly outweigh benefits should be prohibited. How those limits and lines can be determined is a matter where both technical data and moral conscience are needed.

3. The definition of "neighbor" to be cared for includes both near and far neighbor, far in space and time. Therefore justice in the distribution of energy resources must have a care less for my affluent American life-style of consumption and more for that child in the

African hamlet or the citizens of Calcutta. Moreover, the energy
needs of posterity must be weighed into the scales of policy decision.
Should the needs of those in the twenty-first century be sacrified to
satisfy my present wants? The Christian answer here is clearly "No."
For we are accountable to God in the present for neighbors not yet
born.

4. Finally, a distinction must be made, on moral rather than technical grounds, between human needs and human wants. The high
priests of scientism intone a solemn chant celebrating "United Technologies, a continuing response to the needs of life." But if truth be
told, much of the energy used in America is expended on artificial
wants, gadgets, gimmicks, frills, and toys to keep us amused. Might
not the millions that were spent in shooting men and women into
empty spaces have been better spent in filling the empty spaces
within us? Surely, much energy is expended to meet real human
needs: clothing, shelter, lighting, heating, powering hospitals, clinics,
and schools. But much is also expended on needless wants. The ethical question continually must be posed in all of the decisions: is it
energy expended toward humanizing or dehumanizing ends, to create artificial wants or to meet genuine needs? The options posed are
never neat and clean, but always ambiguous. Space satellites provide
valuable knowledge about weather, for example, that meets a human
agricultural need. But to land men on the moon: what good purpose
was served by that feat? Radio communication can save the lives of
folk stranded at sea, or assist in the safe landings of aircraft. But it
can also pollute the air with junk noise and desensitize the soul to
real beauty. Yet within the "grays" of choice, to opt for needs over
wants is to obey the norm of Christian justice and be faithful to the
ethics of the cross.

The Blessings of Austerity

Whatever federal legal measures are enacted to meet the energy
crisis, there is one arena of decision in the private sector where energy consumption can be reduced. We are all consumers, making at
least 100 decisions a day, at home or the office or plant, about light
switches, water faucets, diet, temperature gauges on the water

heater, washing machines, waste disposal, glass bottles, driving, thermostats, etc., etc. The moral imperative is clear: waste less, conserve more. Adopt a simpler life-style. Wait a minute, says the realist, that's ridiculous. What difference does it make to turn off a light switch at home where it's not needed? It would be like a teaspoonful of water added to or taken from Lake Michigan. The single conservationist action is minuscule, yes, but cumulatively, a large difference may be made when a large number of persons make a large number of decisions to conserve energy. The projected line of a 4% annual energy increase can be reduced by concerted, common conscientious effort.

But look, replies the conservative economist, to reduce consumption and lower the GNP would spell economic disaster, massive unemployment, and an intolerable welfare load for the government to carry. It's boom or bust. To which other economists reply, with E. F. Schumacher, that a no-growth, or limited-growth economy need not mean unemployment.[7] Rather, it means the deployment of production from useless to needful goods and services, where "intermediate" technologies are decentralized, and more personal meaning given to the work processes.

Against the American axiom that "more is better" should be pitched the Christian axiom, "enough is enough." There are blessings in conservation and austerity. Physical blessings: a simpler diet without junk foods means the loss of excess weight. Result: better health and longer life. Aesthetic blessings: the recovered vision of the beauty of nature seen when you walk or cycle. But the chief blessing is an inward and moral one that derives from obedience to the sign of the cross: a reduction in our wasteful consumption of energy makes available more of the yield of the earth to meet the crises of world hunger. One simple illustration: Beef is a standard item on the American dinner table. It takes seven pounds of grain to produce one pound of beef. Meatless meals, even if for only one or two days of the week, might free the grain we produce for human rather than animal consumption, and thus, sent abroad under church auspices or a federal food shipment policy, serve to alleviate somewhat the terrible problem of world hunger. The moral ground for the new asceticism, and a simpler life-style, is not that of the monk who would deprive his body to prepare his soul for heaven. Nor is it the Yankee rationale for frugality: to gain wealth. Rather, it is the Biblical moral logic that by cutting back on consumption one may better fulfill responsibility to the far neighbor, "to feed the hungry and clothe the naked," to redistribute the earth's resources more equitably. As one Western delegate to the 1976 Conference of the World Council of Churches at Nairobi put it, "We must learn to live more simply, that others may simply live."

Alternative Energy Sources

Again the voice of practical realism might break in here to say that conservation of itself cannot resolve the energy dilemma. Most Americans are so addicted to high energy use, and the structure of our economy is so geared, that at best we could expect from conservation only a moderate decline in energy use. There are telling minority exceptions. Some small cities like Davis, California (population 38,000) by local ordinances and building codes and public commitment have taken energy conservation seriously. There are more bicycles than automobiles there. Per capita reduction of electricity use since 1973 has been 8%.[8] But by and large American consumers have not accepted the president's word that this is "the moral equivalent of war," partly because the enemy is so invisible, but mostly because we worship the wheel rather than the cross.

Therefore, it is imperative to pursue alternative energy sources. Among the live options, solar energy is the most promising, measured by the moral criteria of stewardship stated above. It is inexhaustible and non-polluting. There are complex technical problems involved in developing solar energy, not the least of which is the requirement of vast land space for heat-collector systems. Yet both scientific and popular support is rising for this alternative, as witnessed by the celebration of Sun Day in May of 1978.[9] Energy derived from winds and water also holds promise. But the sophisticated technology necessary in research and development of energy from the sun, tides, and winds is not sufficiently advanced to hope to make extensive use of them soon. That lead-time gap may be filled by more extensive use of coal, if anti-pollutants like "scrubbers" and strict measures for environmental restoration can be enforced, to preserve the health of miners and the terrain from devastation. And both of these are costly.

In the immediate decades ahead, until power from the sun and tides and wind can be harnessed, nuclear energy plants will be needed. But the decisions about the *type* of nuclear power developed are ethically crucial. From the standpoint of human safety, economy, and health, it seems clear that conventional reactors are morally preferable to breeder reactors and that both a strict prohibition against recycling of plutonium and more stringent measures in the storage of nuclear waste are in the long-term public interest.

In 1976 the National Council of Churches adopted a policy statement calling for a "moratorium on decisions to pursue plutonium reactors as a major energy source." The reaction of the average member in a local congregation—if he or she should even hear of this resolution—would probably be, "The Church should not pass judgment in such scientific and political matters. It should stick to its business of religion. That means faith, worship, prayer, sin, salvation by God's grace, the new life in Christ."

But the NCC statement was a serious attempt to show how the classic doctrines of the Christian faith bear inevitably upon life in a technological culture, and how the ethics of the cross becomes normative for human decisions on how the wheels of technology may be turned for human good and save us from self-destruction.

8

The Earth
Is the Lord's

America is now sauntering through her resources and
through the mazes of her politics with easy nonchalance;
but presently there will come a time when she will be
surprised to find herself grown old—a country crowded,
strained, perplexed—when she will be obliged to fall back
upon her conservatism, obliged to pull herself together,
adopt a new regimen of life, husband her resources, con-
centrate her strength, steady her methods, sober her
views, restrict her vagaries, trust her best, not her average, members. This will be the needed time of change.
Woodrow Wilson

The energy crisis discussed in the previous chapter is only one
facet of a larger erupting problem: the environmental crisis. In the
latter part of the twentieth century, the technical and moral
problems of ecology are pressing in on the public consciousness with
desperate and inescapable urgency. Perhaps thirty years ago, in the
popular mind, the word "ecology" referred to the worries of a few
animal lovers or naturalists, "them ecology freaks," concerned for the
survival of the roseate spoonbill, or the bison, or caribou, or some
other endangered species way off there in the wilds. Few persons had
the prophetic vision of a Woodrow Wilson, in the quotation above, to
see the perils in the paths America was going. (His words were writ-
ten in 1889! What would he write today?)

The acceleration of our destructive powers over nature has now
made a wider public aware that the locus of the ecological problem is
not in Alaska but up and down the streets where we live, that ecological matters become the burden of every person, as producer, as consumer, at the office, at home, in all work and play—though, to be

sure, from the way Americans behave, it does not appear that they really have taken the matter much to heart.

This ecological aspect of the technological revolution—the manner in which the human use of technology has drastically changed our relationship to the natural environment—requires again a close attention to all the empirical facts and the values at stake in them, before we consider the normative response obedient to what the Christian faith asks—indeed, requires—if the human race is to survive.

When one takes a historic overview of the impact of technology on the face of the earth, it is obvious that long before the scientific revolution, wheels and tools of all sorts were used to provide food, clothing, shelter, to travel, and to build temples and tombs, pyramids and palaces, hovels and bridges. But in a pretechnological age, the tools used barely scratched the surface. The rich bounties of earth and sea, of forest and land and the ores below the earth's surface, were hardly touched by stone axe or wooden hoe. There were only a few people scratching: at the beginning of the Christian era some 300 million on the earth, a sparse population compared to the 4 billion plus who now crowd the planet. Even up through the mid-nineteenth century, the pioneer American, migrating west, taming its wilderness with axe and saw, turning forest into farmland, saw nature as a vast inexhaustible resource to be exploited for whatever human needs and wants were desired.

But in this century, the high population density has demanded more and more of the earth. Sophisticated technologies, replacing hoe with bulldozer, club with rifle and then bomb, shovel with deep-sea oil drill, have more than scratched the face of the earth: they have gouged and defaced it. Our human balance with nature has been thrown seriously out of kilter, so seriously in fact, as to threaten all life on earth with a gradual, deadly holocaust.

A new version of the Biblical eschatological close of history begins to appear likely. No longer need we envision one where the trumpet will sound and the heavens will open and the Son of Man will come to judge the quick and dead, or even a mass genocide by nuclear weapons from which the only survivors will be those living in the spaceship satellites, or perhaps a few Eskimos. Rather, the human story may end when the last man staggers out of the last McDonald's and drops finally to death on the asphalt, poisoned by the mercury in his hamburger (the 78 billionth) and the exhaust fumes of his car, whimpering with his last breath, "Well, we blew it, man."

The great eco-system of interdependence among all forms of organic life and inorganic matter (or, to use Christian terms, "the order of creation") is both resilient and delicate, strong and vulnerable. It has its inherent recuperative power, as forests grow back and streams clear themselves eventually from even severe pollution. On the other hand, an injury to one part hurts many other parts, as the lines of Francis Thompson put graphically:

> When to the new eyes of thee
> All things by immortal power,
> Near or far,
> Hiddenly
> To each other linkèd are,
> That thou canst not stir a flower
> Without troubling a star.[1]

If such a poetic metaphor seems a preposterous hyperbole, consider the ruling of the federal Food and Drug Administration against aero-spray cans. When of a morning I press the top of the shaving cream can and it goes "pffft," that innocent deed, I am warned, when done by many, somehow reduces the thickness of the ozone layer encircling the earth, which in turn increases the likely incidence of cancer for my grandchildren. So aero-spray cans are banned. Or when toxic mercury is found in the intestines of penguins in Antarctica, the interaction of all strands of the great web of the eco-system, for good or ill, is empirically confirmed.

The Defacing of Earth

One must be careful here, in fidelity to the facts and values, to present a balanced picture of both the benefits to humanity that technology has wrought and its harms. Scientific prophets of doom, the technophobes, produce a bill of particulars to support their claim that in agriculture the use of pesticides like DDT produces a "silent spring," where no birds call. The technophiles, on the other hand, point to the tremendous human benefits in the use of poisons that eliminate such deadly diseases as malaria and yellow fever which are transmitted by insects.

The agricultural industry, under the demand for more food for more hungry mouths—thousands every day—cannot wait for the slower economies of nature to rebuild its own soil, but must use chemical fertilizers and pesticides for quick yield. But this human good has been bought at a high moral price. In the trade-off, the cost in human health, the draining of the soil, and the savage tears in the fabric of the eco-system, seem to be as high as the benefit.

Second, the petrochemical industry poses another threat to the eco-system.[2] That industry has grown in the United States at an annual rate of about 8%, a pace outrunning all other manufacturing industries. Its alchemy mixes crude oil and natural gas to turn out all kinds of miracles: detergents for soap, synthetic fibers for cotton and wool, plastics for metal, wood, and glass. Fabricated foods and seasoning, synthetic drugs and toiletries flood the market. Cotton and wool were the main textiles in America up until very recently; now, 70% of textiles are synthetic fibers. But, as with so many tricks of the alchemist, petrochemicals prove to be a mixed blessing. The toxic impact of petrochemicals and the waste products of their manufacture increase the incidence of cancer in the areas where petrochemical plants are located. Even such an innocent sweetener as saccharin now proves dangerous and is likely to be prohibited by the FDA when more evidence is in.

Third, perhaps the most visible form of the impact of the machine on the environment is the growth of the giant kingdom of the automobile. In not much more than half a century, the whole system of transportation in America has been preempted by the internal-combustion-engine-driven Car and all the attendants in the court of His Majesty the Automobile: the vast network of concrete and asphalt highways and cloverleaves, the pipelines and the petroleum barges needed to power more and more cars, the service stations, the parking garages and areas required to wait on His Lordship. An estimated 25% of American industry is involved in manufacturing, retailing, servicing, and highway maintenance for the automobile. In 1967, there were 97 million gasoline-powered vehicles in the United States. In 1975, about 134 million.[3] At the rate of pres-

ent increase, in 1980 there will be 150 million. The vehicle population is increasing three times as fast as the human population. All
these cars ride on about 5 million miles of highway, with a traffic
density of about 25 cars per mile, using about 80 billion gallons of gas
annually, and emitting fumes of carbon monoxide that account for
about 60% of the air pollution hovering over the landscape and taking its high toll of human lives through lung cancer and emphysema.
Add to this the number of persons injured and killed in accidents.
Despite all of the safety measures technology has built into cars and
onto highways, the annual death rate is over 50,000. With the rapid
rate of turnover, about seven million are scrapped each year, pollut-
ing the landscape with additional solid waste. The cost-benefit in recycling the steel in junked cars proves hardly worth the expense.[4] Yet
the automobile industry has become so powerful a political force that
its lobbying clout has succeeded in postponing strict enforcement of
the measures in the Clean Air Act controlling the emission of pollu-
tants. Meanwhile the media daily proclaim the doctrine that the pos-
session of a new automobile is practically as sacred a right as any in
the Bill of Rights of the Constitution.

The cost to the earth of high living in America is very difficult to
measure in statistics, and the moral cost impossible to quantify.
American industry believes it can raid the earth and pay nothing
back in return. But in the invisible system of "social cost accounting"
(or, to use theological terms, "the judgment of God"), the price in
human suffering and the degradation of life is paid by consumer and
producer alike. It is an ecological law that "there is no such thing as a
free lunch." It is evident that high consumerism requires a continued
plundering of the planet for the raw materials that produce all the
gadgets and goodies needed for our convenience and drive the
wheels of the machines that make, sell, deliver, and power them.
Then their waste products have to be dumped back onto the earth.
Each year Americans throw away about 50 billion empty cans, 30
billion glass containers, 4 million tons of plastics, a million TV sets.
Phrases like "throwaway" or "waste disposal" are euphemisms. For
matter is indestructible. Technology may change the form of matter
but not its amount (unless you consider the nuclear conversion of
matter to energy as an exception). Thus our present economy means

inevitably the pollution of the landscape with solid waste, the
streams and oceans with chemical waste killing marine life, and the
air with smog. In 1893, Katherine Lee Bates could write a lyric to
"America the Beautiful" and praise "Thine alabaster cities gleam,
undimmed by human tears." Who lately has seen an alabaster city in
America?

When one stands away from a look at America alone to view the
ecological crisis in global perspective, another factor immediately
comes to sight: the population explosion. Though we have managed
to bring zero population growth to the United States, the number of
people in the world increases exponentially. In chapter 3 I referred to
the ominous fact that at our present rate of growth by the year 2000
there will be two persons standing where now there is one. What
does that augur for human well-being, through the shrinkage of social
space and land space to produce food for such a crowded planet?
Technology in agriculture has increased the yield of the earth in food
enormously, but its rate cannot keep pace with the demands of more
and more hungry mouths. Also, technology in medicine and health
care has lowered the death rate drastically, thus adding longer life for
more and more millions. On the other hand, technology has provided
the means of reducing the birth rate, through contraceptive devices,
vasectomies, etc. But in fact the technical measures to limit birth
have been most used in countries where food is most ample and least
used in the poorer portions of the world where food is most scarce.

Humanity Against the Environment

In this ecological fix, there are certain values on a collison course.
Most of these conflicts are variations on the theme often sounded in
these pages: the good life, as it is defined by the religion of scientism
and capitalism, against the good earth and the fullness of its beauty.

There is also a social dimension to the value conflicts raised in the
ecological crisis. The imbalances of humanity with nature mean that
the benefits to some exact painful costs to others in an economy of
scarcity. When I misuse the earth unduly for my comfort, someone
else has to suffer. Such a moral anomaly appears, for example, with
automobiles. On the one hand, every adult in America feels that he

or she ought to have at least one car to drive. At the same time, no
sensible adult would want the kind of environmental situation and
consummate traffic jam that would obtain if everyone drove a car. In
the same way, every growing city wants to expand its airport facilities. Yet the residents of no neighborhood in the suburban belt want
to have the noise and traffic of the airport in *their* backyards. Let
someone else suffer for what will convenience me. And as for solid
waste disposal, let the city council find another place than *our* neighborhood for dumping the garbage we spew. But if every neighborhood the circle round took this line, the city would face an insoluble
problem.

The "time" dimension of the ecological crisis must also be seen.
If our high-consumption economy demands the use of unreplenish-
able natural resources—and if the population continues to grow—it is
inevitable that despite the cleverest and most extensive developments of technology, posterity must pay a price of suffering and starvation for our present comfort. Easy life now is pitched against
survival-life to come. "Buy now, pay later" would be an ecologically
disastrous policy. "There are no frontiers in present-day pollution
and destruction of the biosphere. Mankind shares a common habitat.
We have mortgaged the old homestead, and nature is liable to fore-
close."[5]

A Christian Response to the Ecological Crisis

In the debate about the factors and forces, both inner and outer,
that have brought American culture to this impasse, there have been
many surmises about who is to blame for despoiling the garden of
Eden. One well-known theory, posed by Professor Lynn White, is
that Biblical Christianity itself is the root of the trouble. According to
White's thesis the commands of God to Adam and Eve in the garden,
to " 'Be fruitful and multiply,' " to " 'fill the earth and subdue it,' " to
" 'have dominion over the fish of the sea and over the birds of the air
and over every living thing' " (Gen. 1:28) have given Christian blessing to human exploitation of a desacralized nature—unlike other religious traditions of the East, in which nature is revered. Since the
"orthodox Christian arrogance toward nature," he says, is one of the

deep religious roots of our trouble, "the remedy must also be essentially religious": an inner change of heart. He proposes as a preferable model St. Francis, who would "depose man from his monarchy over creation and set up a democracy of all God's creatures."[6]

I can agree with White's thesis that the ecological crisis cannot be resolved merely by the tinkering of more technology and that an inner change of will or heart guiding the uses of technology is needed for the resolution of the problem. But his generalization must be challenged sharply that orthodox Christianity is the villain of the piece. For there are other strands in the Biblical tradition and the forms of Christian ethical thought that come from the Bible that inspire ecological responsibility. It is true that the main preoccupation of historical Christian ethics has much more to do with interpersonal relations than with human relations to nature. But ever since Adam and Eve in the garden of Eden were charged by the Creator to "till it and keep it," the norm of stewardship of soil has been a dominant motif.

The ethics of stewardship rests on certain crucial aspects of the Christian doctrine. The first is that "the earth is the LORD's, and the fulness thereof." (Ps. 24:1) The whole eco-system, the continual handiwork of God's creative will, is a glorious interdependent system of organic with inorganic matter. In the order of creation, there is no moral line dividing "good spirit" from "bad matter." In its created essence, "whatever is, is good," as St. Augustine said. But it all belongs to God. Humanity does not own the earth or its yield. Strictly speaking, classical Christian ethics has no doctrine of "private property," as that term is usually understood today. The ethics of property in the classic tradition is "private property for common use." The earth is entrusted by the Creator to persons for them to guard, to protect against abuse, to cultivate responsibly in order to serve human needs. The governing doctrine of stewardship does not mean that nature is to be worshiped as divine, as in some forms of nature-mysticism, any more than it means that nature is to be despised as demonic. Rather—to repeat what was said in the previous chapter on energy—the Christian norm is this: nature is to be used for the service of neighbor out of reverent and grateful love of God. This is the Christian basis for an ecological conscience.

There is obviously an enormous distance between this ideal and its translation into policies and practices. When it comes down to hard choices about strip-mining, selective versus clear-cutting in forest management, landfill and zoning policies in the city, legislation controlling exhaust emission or proscribing certain pesticides, then the options open are always morally ambiguous, falling out between the lesser of two evils. The bumper-sticker "Your Environment: Love It or Lose It" is well meant but puts the choice quite too simply. A Franciscan living today would be quite baffled in trying to love all the animals and "Sister Water, Brother Fire, and Mother Earth" equally. Nor does Albert Schweitzer's principle of "reverence for life" assist very much either, since though I may love all that is alive, I am of necessity required to take some forms of life that other preferred forms may live and grow.

Yet there are some intermediate guidelines derived from this norm of stewardship that can inform ecological decisions. One is that humanity is to *use* the resources of earth, but not *abuse* or use them up. Here the overwhelming moral concern is for the good of posterity. But why should I be concerned that my grandchildren and their children might be starved out because I have lived so comfortably? I won't be here to feel the gnaw of their suffering. In the last analysis, the moral ground for my conservation of present resources for future use is the Christian norm of neighbor-love, holding me accountable to God for the well-being of neighbors yet to be born. It is possible to see how this standard of conservation becomes pertinent to policies on forest maintenance, soil rebuilding, crop rotation, dam-siting, anti-pollution laws such as the Toxic Substances Control Act (1976), and the limiting or permissive policies set by the Environmental Protection Agency.

Enough Is Enough

Another guideline to be derived from the norm of stewardship is that the resources of earth are to be used to serve real human needs more than artificial human wants. Of course, no ethicist of sound mind would propose here a legal laundry list of 12, 15, or 78 human needs for which natural resources may be employed and then 162 items of artificial wants that should be banned. Bare necessities of food, clothing, and shelter do not exhaust the wherewithal for humane living, since persons need beauty as much as bread to be fully human. But it surely is an offense to ethical sensitivity that the luxurious level of consumption in America should go on while in the world around ten thousand persons die daily from the lack of food. A *New Yorker* ad offers a centerpiece by Buccellati of two tropical fishes sculpted in sterling silver for $14,000 the pair. Four pages further on is an appeal from the Christian Children's Fund asking from the reader $15.00 per month to help save a child's life in Africa, whose wistful eyes look up in longing. It would be interesting to know how many respondents there are to each of these ads.

It would also be instructive to know how much the citizens of such major cities in Ohio as Cleveland and Toledo gladly pay per year for liquor as compared to how much they have refused to pay in consistently voting down tax levies to keep their public schools from bankruptcy and closing down.

"Give me neither poverty nor riches; feed me with the food that is needful for me, lest I be full, and deny thee, and say, 'Who is the LORD?' or lest I be poor, and steal, and profane the name of my God." (Prov. 30:8–9)

This prayer in Proverbs reflects a conscience sensitive to the difference between genuine needs and artificial wants. A responsible stewardship of the earth would both change the life-style of the consumer in private decisions made about what is purchased and how it is used, and change public policy through legislation to guard against the continuous plundering of the planet.

There are many students of ecology who claim that the most serious trouble in contemporary economic practices derives not as much from the diminishing resources of the earth as from the inequities in the distribution of the resources we have. The enormous problems of the population explosion and world hunger, with the increasing gap between the overdeveloped nations and the developing nations, will not be solved by the philanthropic gifts of Americans, good though they are, nor by appeals to citizens of the poor nations to stop having children. In such a country as India, faced with a high death rate and with starvation always near, parents believe that many children, especially sons, mean security later on. The only way in which the widening gap between population and resources of food can be turned from death to life is therefore by the strengthening of the economy of the poor nations to the point where parents can feel secure with small families. In turn, the way to achieve this requires much more than sending emergency food rations to feed the starving, crumbs from American tables. It requires sending the agricultural technologies and personnel needed by the poor nations to develop their own self-sufficient agricultural economies.

During his presidential campaign, President Carter proposed that "the United States should be not the military arsenal but the breadbasket of the world." That proposal is certainly not now being fulfilled. *"U.S. development assistance* [to foreign countries] *for 1975 amounted to no more than one-tenth of 1 percent of our GNP, a cost to each citizen of less than two cents a day."*[7] Compared to federal funds for military purposes, the amount appropriated for economic aid abroad is tiny. For one who would claim to live under the sign of the cross, concrete expression through national legislative action must be given to the Christian concern to maintain peace between the human race and nature, and justice among all people. In a world now economically interdependent, public policies must be pursued which can distribute the resources of earth more equitably. "Give us this day our daily bread." For the Christian, "us" means *all* in the human family. The responsible use of the fullness of the Lord's earth to provide bread for all becomes both the impossible dream and the immediate burning moral imperative.

9
Education: Wisdom or Skills?

> The task of education would be, first and foremost, the transmission of ideas of value, of what to do with our lives. There is no doubt also the need to transmit know-how but this must take second place, for it is . . . foolhardy to put great powers into the hands of people without making sure that they have a reasonable idea of what to do with them.
>
> *E. F. Schumacher*

When Bob, a sophomore at State, arrived home for spring break, his announcement that he had decided to major in philosophy was greeted with an emphatic lack of enthusiasm by his family. His father, an insurance salesman, could only explode, "Look, Bob, what can you *do* with philosophy? You can never get a job as a philosopher."

This exchange leads us to the exploration of this chapter on the ethical issues lying behind Bob's decision and his father's protest, an exchange signaling a host of problems in the spirit and drift of American education today.

I have traced the ways in which technology has transformed the outer environment and the inner ethos of American culture in several different sectors. Certainly one such area profoundly influenced by the technological revolution has been education, primary, secondary, and higher. Though we may harbor the illusion that educators are out in front, *leading* the culture in the direction it should go, an honest realism must acknowledge that in fact education really *follows* the dominant cultural trends, and of these the technological tide is the strongest. The market demands of a technological society require the abandonment of the old models of classical education suited for an age long past and the development of new models of education in the skills and techniques suited to operate efficiently all the machineries and systems technology has devised. This conversion from classical to technical education appears on every hand. In the factors to be considered in choosing a college, for example. Or in planning a "two-track" high-school curriculum, providing for college-bound students the more traditional courses in the "liberal arts," and for vocational students, likely to terminate their education with high school, a technical curriculum that can land them a job. But something is lost whatever track you take. It is not a matter of deciding that Homer is more essential than Home Economics. As the above quotation from Schumacher suggests, it is a perilous split either to educate in "know-how" with no attention to "know-what-for," or to educate persons in wisdom who know nothing of how to cope with their technological culture.

At the college level, debates rage in state legislatures about the apportionment of funds: should they go to the technical institutes, or to the liberal arts colleges? Or at a private college or university in a financial bind: which sectors should be cut when something has to go —English Literature, fine arts, social sciences, foreign languages, physical sciences?

The Secularization of Education

The history of higher education in America is the story of the erosion of a Christian philosophy of education by a gradual seepage from a new secular faith that earlier I have identified as the religion of scientism. Almost all the earliest colleges, like Harvard and William and Mary, were established to educate the clergy, as leaders of thought and life in the community. Well up through the latter part of the nineteenth century, colleges east and west were founded and sustained under Christian auspices. The typical curriculum of the early New England college was a tight sequence of Greek, Latin, history, natural science, English, Bible, etc., with a senior integrating course in "Moral Philosophy," taught by the president of the college, a clergyman.

Given these religious purposes, required chapel was taken for granted as an integral part of the education of the whole person, heart as well as mind, and perpetuated even well into the twentieth century at many schools. But when God had faded into an "oblong blur" somewhere up above the altar, compulsory chapel was protested by students as a form of involuntary incarceration and soon abandoned.

At the outset, religious purpose also informed the development of the land-grant (or "tax-supported") colleges. As the Northwest Ordinance of 1787 put it, "Religion, morality, and knowledge, being necessary to good government and the happiness of mankind, schools and the means of education shall forever be encouraged."

The nineteenth century saw the rapid rise of public schools at the primary and secondary levels, officially "secular" in the sense that they were under no sectarian control, yet unofficially religious in that the content of the curriculum was drenched with Christian ethical values and norms. McGuffey's Readers, the standard diet, instructed the young in the Puritan virtues of godliness, charity, sobriety, frugality, prudence, civility. These were presumed to be the sinews of a civil society. All who were to be responsible American citizens should be trained to walk in the paths of righteousness for his name's sake who was Lord God of the universe and close monitor of the human heart.

In the twentieth century, strong secularizing forces began to prevail. The population explosion and the waves of immigration of all sorts of ethnic groups, Christian and non-Christian, challenged the informal Protestant establishment. Supreme Court rulings interpreted the First Amendment clause to mean not only "disestablishment" of any one church, its original intent, but the exclusion of religion entirely from public education, a strict religious neutrality.

> Neither a state nor the Federal Government . . . can pass laws which aid one religion, aid all religions, or prefer one religion over another. . . . No tax in any amount . . . can be levied to support any religious activities or institutions, whatever they may be called, or whatever form they may adopt to teach or practice religion.[1]

By such legal decrees, there was built in the popular mind the notion of a "wall of separation" excluding Christian teaching from the public schools in which almost all American youths were enrolled.

No question was raised, however, about the legality of nurturing young people in the religion of scientism that found many ardent advocates and evangelists among the teachers. Currently, at the college level, HEW scrupulously withholds funds from the use of buildings for "sectarian" purposes but has no qualms about awarding funds for science labs that are becoming the "secular cathedrals" of the modern university. To be sure, recent court rulings have upheld the legality of teaching courses "about" religion in tax-supported universities. Departments of religious studies are numerous, offering courses in "The Bible as Literature," or "Religions of the World." But presumably this instruction must not be evangelical or tainted with proselytism.

In primary and secondary schools, the context of ethnic and religious pluralism in pupil enrollments—Jewish, Christian, Buddhist, Hindu, etc.—precludes the celebration of any one faith as speaking for all. It is the better part of wisdom just to leave the whole matter out and preserve a silent if polite neutrality, referring religious instruction to home and church, where like as not it is haphazard, scanty, and poor. Actually, such neutrality does not have a neutral impact, for the impression is left that religion is of little or no significance or worth in the education of the whole person.

A high moral price is being paid for this sort of secularization. The increased cheating, stealing, plagiarism, mugging, arson, destruction of property, the loss of order and discipline that plague especially the inner-city schools are signals of a serious moral breakdown and the loss of the ethics of civility and of consciences schooled to care for persons and property. The decline in English literacy in SAT scores is less alarming than the decline in the moral literacy of responsibility.

The strength of the technological tide is seen in the shift in curriculum in primary and secondary education from the traditional to technical courses. Also college enrollments have shifted from the private liberal arts colleges to the public universities (currently about 78%, as against 22% in private colleges and universities) and, in the last two decades, to community colleges and technical institutes bursting at their seams, where enrollment figures now match and may surpass enrollments in state and private colleges and universities. Of course, there are many factors explaining this tidal wave beyond the appeal of scientism as against the humanities: the lower cost in attending a nonresidential school, for one, and the pressures of a market economy where more and more persons compete for fewer and fewer jobs.

From the public schools the economies of an urban technological society demand that graduates be trained in specific skills rather than that they be persons versed in the classical subjects—the literature, history, and arts of the Judeo-Christian culture of the West. In the squeeze of a tight, competitive economy, where the unemployment rate hovers between 6% and 7% and ranges much higher for "unskilled" workers (30% to 40% for black youths), in the fierce battle for scarce jobs, it is only sensible for a teenager to acquire skills as a secretary, mechanic, or dental assistant, rather than learn the aesthetic significance of James Joyce's *Ulysses* or the Biblical allusions in Milton. Driver's Ed is more valuable in a car-driven culture than mysticism in a care-driven culture. A course in cosmetology at the technical institute downtown can land you a job; a course in cosmology in the philosophy department at old Crestwood on the hill will not. It will not avail even a college graduate dangling a Phi Beta Kappa key before the secretary in the Employment Assistance Office to allow that she knows the sources of the Russian Revolution, the ontological argument for the existence of God, and *"Je parle Français tres bien."* To one offering those credentials the secretary's cool reply will be, "Please fill out this form sheet, and we'll keep your name on file."

So it is that the older values conveyed in classical education: breadth of vision, the cool of a far historical perspective on near events, a sense of abiding curiosity, wonder, and reverence before the infinite mystery of the universe, a moral wisdom about the uses to which human tools are to be put, the life-perspective of the person who, in Matthew Arnold's famous phrase, "saw life steadily and saw it whole"—all these are endangered if not lost entirely in a technical education that produces persons of tunnel vision, of narrow scope of competence, and scanty imagination.

There is a further problem built into this form of technical education: namely, so rapid is the development of technology that persons trained to operate one type of machine are soon outdated and have to be retrained or let go. Machines keep running ahead of those who are schooled to operate them. This rapid obsolescence of training in the technical field is one of the major sources of anxiety and of insecurity in the employment market. It makes for a sense of personal obsolescence and a loss of the sense of self-worth and self-reliance.

Higher Education Turns Technical

Under these same pressures, the curriculum of the established liberal arts colleges and universities is being turned in a preprofessional direction, so that courses and majors are chosen chiefly with an eye to admission to law, medical, or business schools. As a consequence, courses in aesthetics and literature shrivel and foreign languages perish from the catalogue. At the higher level of professional education, something of the same trend can be seen. A technical ethos of efficiency supplants the ethos of civility rooted in religious faith that once, at least in theory, made the professions of medicine, law, theology, and business callings of service, and education in them an exercise in humane learning.

Medical education poses a most troublesome problem. The amount of technical knowledge needed these days to equip the physician is overwhelming. Instruction in the humanistic aspects of medicine, such as medical ethics, is given low priority. The tendency of medical schools is to produce the technician, the specialist, who sees the patient as a case of emphysema only, not as whole person. Few M.D.'s today have the broad wisdom of the general practitioner.

Legal education, too, has been shifted in purpose from the ethics of civility to the ethics of technical efficiency. The claim was made by a prominent law school dean that the law is "the last liberal art," and that the statement of Alexander Stephens a century ago still holds true:

> The lawyer's province is to aid in the administration of justice, to assist the oppressed, to uphold the weak, to contend against the strong, to defend the right, to expose the wrong,

to find out deceit and to run down vice and crimes of all grades, shades, and characters.

The training given today in a law school bears as much resemblance to this ideal as the life-styles on a typical American campus bear to the words of its alma mater, sung once annually at Commencement. Most of legal education is training in positive laws, precedents and procedures, sophistries to make the worse appear the better reason, and the ways to hide in the gaps between legality and morality. Little attention is given to ethics and jurisprudence. One of the aftermath shocks of Watergate was the realization that those skilled in the law, in high places and low, could so shrewdly subvert justice and make the law a function of power rather than of morality. The American Bar Association, sobered by the Watergate trauma, called for a restoration of ethics as an integral part of legal training. President Carter called those in the legal profession sharply to task for their failure, in catering to the privileged, to serve the purposes of justice. As he put it, "Access to justice must not depend on economic status."

A similar trend can be seen in the other professions such as business administration, training leaders of the business world in the managerial skills to extract maximum profit out of the free competitive economy. Even theological education nurtures its students for "effective" Christian ministry, "effective" defined not as godliness or righteousness but as skill in smooth interpersonal relations, a criterion on which the prophets Amos and Jeremiah would score poorly.

This process of secularization, infusing education with the technical spirit, has had dehumanizing results, or what the scientist calls "negative feedback." In the main, the education producing the highly sophisticated technician, the electronic engineer, the stenographer, the computer monitor, provides these specialists with little knowledge as to how wisely to use the greatly increased leisure which the machine provides. Here again the mixed blessing of technology is evident: it has both liberated and imprisoned the human spirit.

Recovering the Ethics of Civility

What might be a Christian ethical response to all of this? How does one nurture consciences in a technocratic society to become sensitive and wise about the moral ends for which the power of machines should be used? What counter trends can be discerned?

It is heartening to find among educators now strong currents running against the tide I have described. Just as the "Back to Basics" movement in primary education is attempting to raise the level of literacy in reading and writing, so there also has been a move to reintroduce education in ethics back into primary and secondary public schools.

At the primary level, a hopeful new development is the attempt to give children a positive self-concept and a sense of self-worth, as the basis of a sense of interpersonal responsibility. The implicit assumption behind this movement may be a humanistic one or a theological one. But it could well be seen as an example of "secularization" in the good sense of the word—the translation of a New Testament ideal into educational practice: "You are loved and therefore able to love others."

In secondary schools, courses in "Value Clarification" are being introduced more frequently. In the face of the perplexing moral anomie of contemporary society, and its ethnic and religious pluralism, psychologists like Jean Piaget and Lawrence Kohlberg have developed theories of the stages of moral growth useful in interpreting and guiding moral behavior in and out of the classroom. It would be surely a futile exercise in discipline for Mrs. Brown, the sixth-grade teacher, to command her pupils to "be good while I'm out of the room." A precocious one of them might well ask Mrs. Brown, "Ma'am, what does 'being good' consist of, and why should we be good?"

Lawrence Kohlberg's six stages of moral growth are a partial answer to this question. In stages one and two, "right" and "wrong" are defined solely by considerations of their consequences in external rewards or punishments. In the upper stages, five and six, morality becomes a matter of personal autonomous decision; actions are taken because they are seen to be inherently just. A class of sophomores in an inner-city high school are not likely to be dutiful Kantians, all subscribing to the Categorical Imperative because they see its inherent moral logic. And these stages of moral growth by no means automatically parallel the stages of chronological growth. Nonetheless, some growth toward moral maturity and a tender conscience is achieved where value clarification programs are skillfully taught.[2]

Such programs are least effective when taught in isolated abstraction; most effective when integrated with the other subjects of the curriculum, where the student is confronted by the moral issues that lie close underneath all technical decision, private and public. By law, instruction in these programs cannot be "sectarian" or "evangelical." But in consideration of the whole syndrome of American values, the Christian values of compassion, concern for persons, self-sacrifice, and justice for the oppressed are certainly part of the mix, along with the democratic values of equality and the protection of individual rights and freedoms, the capitalistic values of economic growth, competition, individualism, and the scientistic values of comfort, efficiency, speed, and convenience. It is important for a student to see where in this mix the values collide and where they coincide. Incidentally, one of the most difficult but rewarding ways to teach ethics is to use materials from the humanities: great novels (Hawthorne, Tolstoi, Melville) or plays (Shakespeare, Ibsen), or modern films, or the major centerpieces of political history and social science, to alert students to the value collisions and resolutions that are at the heart of these pieces of literature and history.

At the level of higher education, it is noteworthy that educators, troubled too by the loss of the ethics of civility and the moral anarchy of the university mind, and by the strong mind-set of students to regard the four-year liberal arts curriculum as only a preprofessional corridor for getting into medical or law schools, are calling for a return to education in morality. President Derek Bok of Harvard, in a recent Commencement address, asked that more attention be given to the questions of human character, to problem-oriented courses in ethics, classes built around America's moral dilemmas.[3] And in one of his last reports as president of Yale University, Kingman Brewster wrote, "the development of a capacity for moral judgment should be a major aim of liberal education."[4]

In Harvard's new core curriculum of 1978, one course is required in "philosophical analysis," designed to enable students to "think systematically about such issues as justice, obligation, personal responsibility, citizenship, friendship." While such a course may be quite a distance from the statement of the founding purpose of Harvard in 1636: that everyone shall consider "the maine end of his life and studies" to know God and Jesus Christ, "which is eternal life,"[5] it does signal a sober concern for the moral dimension of liberal education.

Moral Wisdom and Technical Skills

The realist will press the question still: how? In what specific directions might education move to instill moral sensitivities and concern, given the demands of a technocratic society? The title of this chapter poses the problem as an option: wisdom *or* skills? But perhaps the answer may be both-and: wisdom *and* skills. As the philosopher Whitehead put it many years ago, "The antithesis between a technical and a liberal education is fallacious. There can be no adequate technical education which is not liberal, and no liberal education which is not technical: that is, no education which does not impart both technique and intellectual vision."[6] Jacques Barzun, protesting the "fruitless debate between so-called useful and so-called useless education," asks for education immediately useful in a bread-and-butter sense to the demands of the economy, and also one "conducive to the individual's enduring *psychic* economy—his ethico-spiritual and esthetic economy—as well as the overarching goals of society."[7] Herein may lie the resolution of the clash between Bob's decision to major in philosophy and his father's protest.

One viable way is to broaden the curriculum in the technical institutes and community colleges to include more courses and experiences in the humanities: art, music, literature, philosophy, religion, drama. The opening of minds to the great perennial questions of truth, beauty, and goodness is not useless but indispensable to the education of the full person to fill out his or her technical training. At one community college in Atlanta, for example, in the Automotive Technology Diploma program, a student may take T.ESP 118: Human Relations *and* T.ETR 111:Hydraulic Brakes. Zen may have a connection with the art of motorcycle maintenance after all! A report some years ago of the Carnegie Commission (*A Degree and What Else?*) showed that graduates of liberal arts colleges and universities were markedly less provincial-minded, both in a temporal and a spatial sense, more ethically responsible in private and public choices, less "engineered" and more deliberate and free in behavior choices than persons who had had only a technical education. For persons schooled in the humanities, the sense of wonder is deepened, the vision is enlarged, and the conscience is alerted to the ends, humane or inhumane, for which the vast powers of technique may be used.

At the still higher levels of education, in professional schools, the measures needed to counter the trend toward efficiency as the single goal would be to supplement the existing technical courses with courses in professional ethics. Legal education, for instance, should grapple with the issues of the relationship of law and power and justice. What wisdom is there in the "natural law" tradition—God's everlasting laws set in the created order and grasped by reason—that has been lost in preoccupation with positive laws? Where does the letter of the law express the spirit of the laws and where does it subvert that spirit?

In medical schools the treatment of the patient as a total person and the questions of humane policy on such morally tangled issues as euthanasia, abortion, cloning, and DNA research must be addressed before the results of research are put into practice. Technology has forced the physician today to "play God" whether he or she would or not. The crucial ethical issue is what best moral wisdom can guide the skills of the machinery and techniques at hand? In the social sciences or "policy sciences," training personnel for administrative posts in business or politics calls for the humanistic perspective, to provide a moral sensitivity to the overarching consideration of common justice.

One scholar puts the case for the humanities this way,

> [The humanities] teach us what it is to be human .... What we gain from them is not an accumulation of facts but an enlargement of our own humanity. They do not guarantee the survival of the species, but they do provide conditions necessary to the life of the spirit. They do not swell the Gross National Product, but they enrich the lives of individuals and deepen the sense of community among men and cultures.[8]

That this claim is not mere rhetoric, to be endured in a Commencement address to the graduating classes perspiring in caps and gowns, is attested by heartening recent evidence. Of the 116 medical schools in the nation, at least half offer programs or courses in medical ethics. In law and engineering schools, ethics courses are also on the marked increase.[9]

Look also at the recent sharp rise in Continuing Education programs all across the nation. Adults from all walks and of all ages, facing the heavy weight of empty leisure that technology has dumped on them and seeking enrichment of life, are enrolling in adult education courses in great numbers. Not only out of economic pressures, where wife and husband both need a paying job to make ends meet, but often for unpragmatic reasons: they are excited by learning art, music, literature, theology, history, philosophy, and the mysteries that modern science illumines. From such a continual growth in learning can come the wisdom needful to redeem life not only from boredom but from the genuine peril of human destruction towards which an inhumane and uncontrolled technology can lure us, like lemmings rushing over the edge of the cliff into the sea.

Such wisdom derived from the humanities might provide an aristocracy of judgment in a democratic society. To speak of "aristocracy" sounds like elitism and snobbishness. But there is truth in the "aristocratic" tradition, as there is fallacy in the democratic faith that quantity of opinion guarantees quality of opinion or, in other words, that you get closer to the truth by counting more noses. Not necessarily so. Democracy is saved from anarchy by the judgment of the aristocracy (not the wealthiest, or the most powerful, but the *aristoi*, the best and the wisest) who bring to public policy decisions care for the dignity and worth of persons, an openness to differences, a trust in the integrity of foe and friend, in short, the ethics of civility. To translate this into Christian terms, civility stems from Christian love, which in turn finds its ground and sanction in the Christian faith.

But the stubborn problem that the realist might raise still remains: instruction *about* morality does not of itself assure that a student, young or old, will adopt the ethics of civility in practice. The mind's vision does not of itself guarantee the will's commitment. For one must acknowledge with St. Paul the perennial distance between knowing better and doing worse. Here perhaps is one of the shortfalls of the value clarification programs I have mentioned. They may assist students to sort out objectively what values are in collision in their culture and in themselves, and what goods they most prize, but this of itself may give no guidance as to which values are prize-worthy or by what norm one set of values should be preferred over another in the inevitable economy of scarcity which sets close limits on everyone's daily living. Thus the teenager may prize highly "independence"—the freedom "to do my own thing," unencumbered by parental hoverings, cautions, and restraints. But *ought* that to be the supreme value—never mind about consideration for parents?

In wrestling with problems of value collisions in society and in one's own life, and in studying the classics of the humanities, one might indeed hope that the searching student would become "existentially" promised to moral action. But factors and forces other than formal education are necessary to develop a caring conscience and a committed will. If there is truth in the old Calvinistic moral norm, "Knowledge is in order to goodness," then whether the educated person tears or strengthens the fabric of community depends not merely on the extent of that person's information but on the sensitivity of his or her conscience. There are many subtle, strong powers educating the conscience and will outside the classroom or library. One, obviously, is the home. Another, less obviously, is the church. But what *can* the church do to humanize technology?

10

The Church as
the Conscience of
a Technical Society

> I simply argue that the Cross be raised again at the center
> of the market place as well as on the steeple of the
> church. . . . that Jesus was not crucified in a Cathedral be-
> tween two candles, but on a Cross between two thieves;
> on the town garbage heap; . . . at the kind of place where
> cynics talk smut, and thieves curse, and soldiers gamble.
> Because that is where He died. And that is what He died
> about. . . . that is where churchmen should be and what
> churchmen should be about.
>
> *George MacLeod*

To try to understand the role of the Christian church in contemporary American society is a bewildering task. Much of the difficulty
comes from a confusion in thought and talk between the descriptive
picture of what the church actually *is* and *does,* such as a sociologist
might form out of empirical evidence, and a normative vision of
what the church *ought* to be, such as the pastor in the pulpit might
preach. One thing is clear: the empirical reality is considerably different from the ideal voiced in the Sermon on the Mount: " 'You are the
salt of the earth. You are the light of the world.' "

It is possible to make some order and sense out of this confusion,
and to explain the distance between the ideal and the actual, by
watching the traffic of influence between the church and the world,
that is, between what is honored and practiced at the altar and what
is honored and practiced in the shopping center, and how they affect
each other. In church the prevailing belief is the evangelical ideal,
the thesis that the church is in the world, converting the world to
Christianity. Presumably the traffic moves from church to world. But

a more careful look would confirm the antithesis, that really the traffic in the opposite direction is much stronger: the world is in the church, converting the church to secularism.

This antithesis is more than just hypocrisy: that the church practices less than what it preaches. It is rather a matter of conflicting loyalties and faiths, wherein church behavior expresses loyalty to other deities than the God of the Christian faith, though this transcendent Lord of the universe is the professed center of value and the ultimate object of faith and trust.

Though not clearly visible, there are many secular deities worshiped at the First Presbyterian Church on the corner of Broad and Main: capitalism, the civil religion of Americanity, hedonism, to name a few. Perhaps the most powerful of the secular deities invading the church is the god of scientism. The standards of value in the currency of social exchange within the church are derived much less from the mind of Christ than from the creed of scientism. Organizational efficiency, quantitative growth in membership and budget, smooth interpersonal functioning, convenience and comfort in the improvement of physical facilities—these are supposed by many to make a church more "Christian." In the enterprising church in Florida that gives out green stamps for church attendance, which is more honored, the cross or the wheel?

The secularization of the churches influences also the concept of the ministry. Throughout Judeo-Christian history, there has been a running debate, starting back in the Old Testament with the collision between priest and prophet, as to whether the church should be comfort or challenge to the society in which it exists, whether it should smooth or ruffle the feathers of the soul. Christ, the Lord of the church, affirmed both. "My peace I give to you," he said, but also "I have not come to bring peace, but a sword." Any Christian church is faithful to its Lord when it both comforts the afflicted and afflicts the comfortable.

Surely the priestly task of the pastor to bring comfort is essential. In every corner of the parish, whether among the affluent or the poor, there are persons lonely, bereaved, lost, confused, embittered, who need the consolation of the grace of God in Christ that the church can provide for both body and spirit. Yet in fact there is a

serious imbalance between the priestly and the prophetic: the ministry of the church is largely preoccupied with healing and comfort,
very little with challenge.

Theological education trains the pastor in counseling, in therapeutic skills, and in the efficient "management of interpersonal relations." The scientism here is evident. Life's dilemmas are translated
from the scenario of sin and salvation to the scientistic drama of
problem and solution, the maladjustments of the various parts of the
social machinery for which psychological devices can be employed to
restore full functioning adjustment. It is Ann Landers with a clerical
collar.

The success of the pastor's preaching is measured by the number
of worshipers who will greet him or her at the door as they leave with
the polite word, "I enjoyed your sermon." (One wonders if anyone
ever told Amos, "I enjoyed your sermon"!) It is politic for the
preacher to heed the hearers of Isaiah who said, " 'Speak to us
smooth things' " (Isa. 30:10), rather than to risk provoking something
like the comment of one salty parishioner who said, as he left the
church after hearing a prophetic sermon, "I was with you, preacher,
until you got specific."

To escape this "suburban captivity," and the popular image of
the church as only a place of refuge or a "House of Happiness," the
first long step toward a synthesis beyond the thesis and the antithesis
would be to affirm a declaration of independence from secularism, to
stand at a good distance from all of the benign and respectable idola-
tries where secular deities pass for Christian, to turn from the worship of the wheel and return to a stance of faith under the sign of the
cross. Such distancing does not mean in the Protestant tradition a
physical withdrawal but a spiritual withdrawal. The sanctuary remains right downtown or in suburbia. Yet it is "in the world but not
of the world" in its center of spiritual gravity. It is committed to a
life-style that runs counter to that of secular society.

The simple radical question must be addressed: what after all *is* a
Christian church that distinguishes it from the country club, the
social-service agency, the counseling clinic, the academy? The normative answer may be given in terms of its distinctive functions and
purposes.

"To Glorify God"

Foremost is worship. The Christian church is a community of persons who celebrate the majesty, power, glory, and grace of God, the Creator, Judge, and Redeemer, as he is known in nature and history, and crucially in the event of Jesus Christ.

The authentic worship of God takes many forms. In liturgy, formal or informal, the community of believers gathers to honor the name of God, in song, in silence, in spoken word, in prayer, in dance, in sacraments, to celebrate the great Goodness at the heart of the great mystery that surrounds human existence. In worship, the essential stance of spirit is reverence, awe, wonder. In that frame of spirit, the classical prayers of traditional liturgy are set: thanksgiving, confession, intercession, petition. In authentic worship, the eyes of the heart are turned away from the machineries and techniques of the community's housekeeping, from budgets and bylaws, from schedules and announcements, toward the ends for which these machineries turn their wheels. In the Reformed tradition, the "chief end of man" is not to balance the budget but "to glorify God and enjoy him forever."

As a community of seekers and believers, the church glorifies God not only when gathered in for formal worship Sunday morning but also when scattered out through the week, in their various jobs, at the factory, at the desk, in the kitchen. It is no less a church when scattered than when gathered. Moreover, it is at these posts in the world that the real test of their loyalty in membership comes. Easy to affirm one's vows to do the will of God on Sunday; much more difficult when confronted on Monday with a morally ambiguous political or business decision. Yet as the Old Testament prophets remind Israel again and again, God is truly worshiped in deeds of justice, righteousness, mercy, in the marketplace. Christ stands squarely in this prophetic tradition. In sharp rebuke to the conspicuous piety of the Pharisees, who observed ritual in minute detail and fussed over all the blue laws of Sabbath-keeping, Jesus' act of healing on the Sabbath was an act of true worship in hallowing the Sabbath and revering God's name.

"With All Thy Mind"

A second function and activity of the Christian church is education. If my definition is correct that the church is a community of believers who seek to hallow the name of God by doing his will in the world, it follows that enlightenment of the mind as to the *content* of that will becomes as necessary as the commitment of the heart, before and while Christians take action.

In the previous chapter I took account of the dangerous imbalance between technical skills and moral wisdom. One largely untapped resource for a recovery of the knowledge of ethics lies in the Christian tradition. We must acknowledge the pathetic fact that what currently goes on in the Christian education program at First Church is thin, casual, perfunctory, and brief. With public education so secularized, and the track record of the churches in education so poor, it is little wonder that most high-school graduates are Biblically, theologically, and ethically illiterate. They may know lots about the atom but have never even heard of Adam. If truth be told, their seniors are not much better informed. And the situation is made worse by the anti-intellectual temper in some conservative evangelical churches, now rising in popularity, which regard the careful and critical study of the Christian tradition somehow as dangerous to true faith. Don't analyze, question, criticize: just *believe.*

Yet if membership in the community of the church entails an obligation to love God "with all thy mind," then a serious and systematic program of education is indispensable. In the Reformed tradition, this would have its base in the study of Scriptures, to establish at least some Biblical literacy. But no Christian education is responsible or sufficient that stops with Bible study, where so often it does. It should build on that foundation to a study of the history of the Christian tradition and to a systematic study of Christian theology and ethics. An adult class made up of seekers willing to articulate their radical doubts as readily as their conventional convictions can make the study of Christian theology and ethics lively and rewarding. What *are* the divine signs to be seen in the turbulent present? How do we interpret them aright for our faithful response? What *did* the phrase "kingdom of God" mean for Luther, Calvin, Jonathan Edwards, Pope John XXIII? What does it mean for us? What *are* the moral terms of the "natural law" tradition? What social policies are implied in the theme of the most recent Conference of the World Council of Churches at Nairobi: "Jesus Christ who frees and unites"? In pursuit of questions like these the class may become versed in the basic themes of Christian theology, bringing to bear moral wisdom on the problems of a technological culture. There is no dodging it: conscience responsible both to the faith and the facts requires an informed mind as much as a committed will.

A Point of Forum for Ethical Exchange

A third major function and task of a prophetic church is to become a *forum* where all the dilemmas forced upon us by the technological revolution are addressed in the light of Christian ethical norms.

The crucial issues in medicine, in the economy, in politics, in communications, reviewed in earlier chapters, are not amenable to solution by mere technical information, because there are human values in collision and options forced that scientific expertise cannot answer. The treasure held in the tradition of the church, though in earthen vessels, is a rich wisdom as to what values should be prized and protected to make and keep human life human. The relevance of Christian ethics to all these dilemmas should be explored in depth.

The hot problems are inevitably controversial. On abortion, homosexuality, "affirmative action," labor-management relations, civil rights, criminal justice—about any one of these conscientious Christians will surely disagree. In a worldly church, leaders back off from addressing them because to do so would cause dissension, disagreement; and above all "we must keep the peace." Such caution is disloyal to what a Christian church should be. It is not a community of agreement like that of the club, but a community of trust among those who may disagree. Their shared trust enables them to listen for the prophetic word of God even when it cuts against their tidy and safe preconceptions.

There are many exciting ways to turn a church into a place of forum. For example, where several members are engaged in professional medicine, they might form a study group on medical ethics. What does the norm of Christian love as care for persons prescribe when laid against the practices of abortion or euthanasia? Or, for those in professional business, what should be the relation of government to the free-enterprise system? It is easy to pledge allegiance to the flag of a nation with "liberty and justice for all," but more difficult to translate into economic policy when liberty and justice seem to collide. In celebrating the value of the free competitive market, we may be blinded to the injustices it brings. As Charles Dickens's quotation put it, " 'Each one for himself and God for us all,' as the elephant said as he danced among the chickens." The value of "freedom" often conflicts head on with "equality," since at first glance the pursuit of unregulated freedom results in gross economic inequalities, while a federally required equality undercuts the individual initiative and freedom which according to conventional wisdom are the mainsprings of a capitalistic economy. How does Christian justice balance these two?

Another chronic problem that besets all members of the community of the church is that of the strength or weakness of the family structure in American culture today. What forces, inner and outer, are at work affecting the nuclear family unit for good or ill? What is the responsibility of parents in the matter of sex education for their teenage children? To counter the influence of the sex-drenched media, how does one nurture the right understanding of sexuality and Christian love? Or what of black-white relations in the schoolyard or on the school board? Are there hidden racial fences in the zoning regulations of your suburb? What about the energy crisis? Or world hunger and the American life-style of consumption?

Doing the Word

Finally, as the fruit and sign of its faithful worship, its schooling in and discussion about the bearing of Christian ethics on contemporary problems, the church should become the center and spring of covenanted, committed action.

In the depths of the individual soul, the role of conscience is a double one: to be both troubler and guide. So for the church as the conscience of a technical society, part of its task is to disturb people through its radical critique, pointing to the disparity between the "is" and the "ought." But the other part is as important: to be guide, pointing its culture toward a better way and prodding folk to follow it. It should witness its convictions of conscience not only within its own walls but outside, publicly, openly, to try to turn public policy to accord with its persuasion of what God's righteousness demands.

Just *how* it should set about "doing the word" in public is a difficult, ambiguous matter. An immediate obstacle is the long-entrenched tradition of separation of church and state, commonly read to mean that the church should steer clear of politics, where it doesn't belong. As a result, most churches are hotbeds of political apathy. As a consequence of this tradition, the scope of Christian morality is narrowed to matters of private behavior. Christian virtue means the avoidance of the sins of the flesh.

Yet the separation of church and state does not and should not mean the separation of morality and politics. Where moral issues of crucial concern for Christians are to be decided in the political arena, then the corporate witness of the Christian community should be voiced. The church should be up to its steeples in politics.

On any particular matter where feelings run high, the church's public stance should express both the courage of its conviction of conscience and a contrition conscious of its own partiality and finitude, making no claim to a monopoly on the whole truth. Difficult indeed to do. Crusaders are not usually contrite. Yet righteousness for the truth need not mean self-righteousness any more than contrition need mean indecision.

On the major vexed issues of current public policy such as the use of nuclear weaponry, the SALT treaties, welfare and tax reform, the role of the state in handling labor disputes, criminal justice, the civil and private rights of homosexuals, it is difficult to decide rightly "who speaks for the church?" Though its voice is never unanimous, there is no other voice that can better speak for the conscience of America.

The insights on these matters discerned in worship and study must body forth in *praxis.* In the life of the local congregation, some will be more controversial, some less, some not political at all. I cite but a few. To strengthen the fragile bonds of family life, and to fill with meaning the empty leisure that technology has created, the church's recreation program may teach its families the almost forgotten art of playing together. A family-centered recreation program can liberate persons from the TV illusion that violence and sex are the only source of excitement. Joy in creativity in the arts, in athletics, in music, in drama, can clear life from the dross of spectatoritis and strengthen the bonds of affection between parents and children.

A particular congregation, or a number among them, may express its ecological conscience by covenanting together to adopt a simpler life-style, to cut down on waste, and to commit a portion of its income to Church World Service, for world hunger. Or perhaps persuade the official board of the church to apportion a larger share of the budget to benevolent causes, less to housekeeping. Or it might make the parish house a recycling center for paper, glass, and aluminum, and recruit its young people to organize a recycling program if there has been none.

Another area of action, more directly political, is that of penal justice. A task force on criminal justice might study what practices prevail in the local courts in the handling of juvenile delinquency, in granting paroles, in sentencing. Does the treatment of persons in the local jail accord with Christian humanitarian concern? What about capital punishment? Where might the church act as a sustaining community to rehabilitate the parolee? How might it reduce the high rate of recidivism?

On the whole issue of civil rights, a church community, although by long custom racially segregated, may learn what new life in Christ is like when it takes a stand for equal justice, for "affirmative action" policies, for ERA, for the representation of minorities on school boards and civic commissions. Its witness will be the more convincing if it can realize integration within its own membership. Its public support of Amnesty International or the American Civil Liberties Union would signal its courage to witness for human rights abroad and at home.

"You are the salt of the earth." There is a double sense in this phrase. In Biblical times, salt was used as a food preservative, a protection against rot and decay. And, of course, salt is a sharp condi-

ment. The metaphor can stand as normative for the role of the
Christian church in an urban technological culture. On the one hand
it serves the conservative function, to preserve the tradition, to keep
true to the old, to prove a reliable guide for responsible action. On
the other hand, it serves a revolutionary function, as sharp bite
against the bland and easy identification of the church with secular
culture. The saving word of God's work in Christ must come as offense before it can be understood as gospel, the good news of human
redemption.

Notes

Chapter 2. From Christian Love to Social Policy
   1. Joseph Fletcher, *Situation Ethics* (Philadelphia: Westminster, 1966), p. 85.

Chapter 3. Matters of Life and Death
   1. *11 Million Teenagers: What Can Be Done About the Epidemic of Adolescent Pregnancies in the United States* (New York: Alan Guttmacher Institute of Planned Parenthood, 1976), p. 32.
   2. One estimate puts legal abortions in the U.S. at about 180,000 per year; illegal abortions (almost impossible to determine) range from 200,000 to over a million. See James B. Nelson, *Human Medicine: Ethical Perspectives on New Medical Issues* (Minneapolis: Augsburg, 1973), p. 33.
   3. Roe v. Wade, 93 Supreme Court 705 (1973), quoted in Nelson, *Human Medicine*, pp. 43-44.
   4. "A Call to Concern," *Christianity and Crisis*, 3 October 1977, p. 222.

Chapter 4. Work and Vocation
   1. Peter Berger, "Some General Observations on the Problem of Work" in *The Human Shape of Work*, ed. Peter Berger (New York: Macmillan, 1969), p. 217.
   2. U.S. Department of Health, Education, and Welfare, *Work in America: Report of a Special Task Force to the Secretary of HEW* (Cambridge, Mass.: MIT Press, 1973), pp. x-xi.
   3. See Elton Mayo, *The Social Problems of an Industrial Civilization* (Boston: Harvard University Press, 1945), pp. 59-112.
   4. Nicolas Herman [Brother Lawrence], *The Practice of the Presence of God* (Mount Vernon, N. Y.: Peter Pauper, 1963), p. 25.
   5. Kenneth Underwood, "On the Pinnacles of Power—The Business Executive" in *The Human Shape of Work*, ed. Peter Berger, p. 201.
   6. Stanley Parker, *The Future of Work and Leisure* (New York: Praeger, 1971), chapter 4.

Chapter 5. The Fulfillment of Leisure
   1. Gordon J. Dahl, "Time, Work and Leisure Today," *The Christian Century*, 10 February 1971, p. 187 (Dahl's italics).

2. See Sebastian de Grazia, *Of Time, Work, and Leisure* (New York: Twentieth Century Fund, 1962), pp. 13-15.

3. George Soule, cited in Robert Lee, *Religion and Leisure in America* (New York: Abingdon, 1964), p. 260.

4. *Ibid.*, p. 17 (Lee's italics).

Chapter 6. The Ethics of Communication

1. Kyle Haselden, *Morality and the Mass Media* (Nashville: Broadman, 1968), p. 141.

2. *Newsweek*, 21 February 1977, p. 64.

3. Malcolm Muggeridge, *Christ and the Media* (Grand Rapids, Mich.: Eerdmans, 1977), pp. 29-30.

4. Robin Day, "Troubled Reflections of a TV Journalist," *Encounter*, May 1970, p. 79.

5. William L. Rivers and Wilbur Schramm, *Responsibility in Mass Communication*, 2d ed. rev. (New York: Harper & Row, 1969), pp. 256–259.

Chapter 7. The Energy Crisis

1. There are mountains of studies, governmental and private, on the scientific side. I have found most useful: (a) the report of the Nuclear Energy Policy Study Group, *Nuclear Power: Issues and Choices*, sponsored by the Ford Foundation (Cambridge, Mass., 1977), (b) the booklets of the League of Women Voters Education Fund, *Energy Dilemmas* and *Energy Options* (1977), and (c) the World Council of Churches reports, "Energy for a Just and Sustainable Society," *Anticipation*, November 1976, and "Report on Nuclear Energy," *Anticipation*, October 1975. See also John Francis and Paul Abrecht, *Facing Up to Nuclear Power* (Philadelphia: Westminster, 1976), and Paul Abrecht, ed., *Faith, Science and the Future* (Philadelphia: Fortress, 1979).

2. Donella H. Meadows et al., *The Limits to Growth* (New York: Universe Books, 1972).

3. V. Lawrence Parsegian, "Nuclear Energy: Its Role in Human Affairs," *Anticipation*, November 1976, p. 18.

4. Nuclear Regulatory Commission, *Reactor Safety Study—An Assessment of Accident Risks in U.S. Commercial Nuclear Power Plants* (October 1975).

5. Union of Concerned Scientists, "What You Should Know About the Hazards of Nuclear Power" (1208 Massachusetts Ave., Cambridge, Mass. 02138).

6. "Energy for a Just and Sustainable Society," *Anticipation*, November 1976, p. 5.

7. E. F. Schumacher, *Small Is Beautiful: Economics as if People Mattered* (New York: Harper & Row, 1973). See also his *Good Work* (New York: Harper & Row, 1979).

8. *Newsweek*, 18 April 1977, p. 74.

9. Barry Commoner, *The Politics of Energy* (New York: Knopf, 1979).

Chapter 8. The Earth Is the Lord's

1. Francis Thompson, "The Mistress of Vision," st. xxii, in *Poems and Essays*, ed. Wilfred Meynell, 3 vols. in one (Freeport, N. Y.: Books for Libraries Press, 1969), 2:9.

2. Barry Commoner, "The Promise and Perils of Petrochemicals," *New York Times Magazine*, 25 September 1977, pp. 38ff.

3. *Statistical Abstract of the United States* (1976), p. 595.

4. Kenneth P. Cantor, "Warning: The Automobile Is Dangerous to Earth, Air, Fire, Water, Mind and Body" in *The Environmental Handbook*, ed. Garrett De Bell (New York: Ballantine Books, 1970), pp. 197ff.

5. Lord Ritchie-Calder, "Mortgaging the Old Homestead," *Foreign Affairs*, January 1970, p. 220.

6. Lynn White, Jr., "The Historical Roots of Our Ecologic Crisis," appearing first in *Science*, 10 March 1967 (the quotations are from pp. 1207, 1206), and often reprinted in other symposia on ecology.

7. Arthur Simon, *Bread for the World* (Grand Rapids, Mich.: Eerdmans, 1975), p. 115 (Simon's italics).

Chapter 9. Education: Wisdom or Skills?

1. Everson v. Board of Education, 330 U.S. 1 (1947).

2. For further references, see Robert T. Hall and John V. Davis, eds., *Moral Education in Theory and Practice* (Buffalo: Prometheus, 1975); Sidney B. Simon, Leland W. Howe, and Howard Kirschenbaum, *Values Clarification* (New York: Hart Publishing Co., 1972); and C. M. Beck, B. S. Crittenden, and E. V. Sullivan, eds., *Moral Education* (Toronto: University of Toronto Press, 1971).

3. *New York Times*, 15 May 1977, p. A1.

4. Kingman Brewster, "Report of the President" (published by Yale University, 1975–76).

5. Quoted in Howard Lowry, *The Mind's Adventure: Religion and Higher Education* (Philadelphia: Westminster, 1950), p. 40.

6. Alfred North Whitehead, "Technical Education and Its Relation to Science and Literature" in *The Aims of Education and Other Essays* (New York: Macmillan, 1929), p. 74.

7. Maxwell H. Goldberg, "Introduction" to *Automation, Education and Human Values*, ed. William W. Brickman and Stanley Lehrer (New York: School & Society Books, 1966), pp. 13, 14.

8. O. B. Hardison, Jr., *Toward Freedom and Dignity: The Humanities and the Idea of Humanity* (Baltimore: Johns Hopkins, 1972), p. xxii.

9. *New York Times*, 20 February 1978, pp. A1, B8.

Index